William Delisle Hay

Brighter Britain!

Settler And Maori in Northern New Zealand

William Delisle Hay

Brighter Britain!
Settler And Maori in Northern New Zealand

ISBN/EAN: 9783744725262

Printed in Europe, USA, Canada, Australia, Japan

Cover: Foto ©ninafisch / pixelio.de

More available books at **www.hansebooks.com**

BRIGHTER BRITAIN!

OR

SETTLER AND MAORI

IN

NORTHERN NEW ZEALAND.

BY

WILLIAM DELISLE HAY,

AUTHOR OF
"THREE HUNDRED YEARS HENCE," "THE DOOM OF THE GREAT CITY," ETC.

> "Queen of the seas, enlarge thyself!
> Send thou thy swarms abroad!
> For in the years to come,—
> Where'er thy progeny,
> Thy language and thy spirit shall be found,—
> If—
> —in that Austral world long sought,
> The many-isled Pacific,—
> When islands shall have grown, and cities risen
> In cocoa-groves embower'd;
> Where'er thy language lives,
> By whatsoever name the land be call'd,
> That land is English still."
> SOUTHEY.

IN TWO VOLUMES.—VOL. II.

LONDON:
RICHARD BENTLEY AND SON,
NEW BURLINGTON STREET.
1882.

CONTENTS OF VOL II.

CHAPTER		PAGE
I.	OUR SPECIAL PRODUCTS	1
II.	OUR CLASSIC GROUND	29
III.	MAORI MANNERS. I.	71
IV	MAORI MANNERS. II.	100
V.	MAORI MANNERS. III.	135
VI.	OUR NATURALIST'S NOTE-BOOK	184
VII.	THE DEMON DOG—A YARN	232
VIII.	OUR LUCK	272
	APPENDIX	303

BRIGHTER BRITAIN!

CHAPTER I.

OUR SPECIAL PRODUCTS.

NORTHERN New Zealand has two special products, which are peculiar to the country, and found nowhere else. They are kauri timber and kauri-gum. When speaking of Northern New Zealand in these sketches, I do not thereby intend the whole of the North Island, as has been previously explained; I mean that northern part of it which may be more properly designated "The Land of the Kauri."

The kauri grows throughout all that part of the old province of Auckland which lies to the north of S. lat. 37° 30′ or 38°. It does not grow naturally anywhere south of the thirty-eighth parallel of latitude, nor, I believe, can it be induced to flourish under cultivation south of its natural boundary line.

The kauri is indigenous to this comparatively

small section of New Zealand. It is one of the *Coniferæ*, or pines, and is named by botanists *Dammara Australis*. The only tree of similar species that affords a timber nearly resembling the kauri, though not of such good quality, is one that is found in Fiji; the *Dammara Vitiensis*. It may be as well to mention that kauri and Maori rhyme together, and are pronounced "kowry" and "mowry."*

The kauri was first brought into notice by Captain Cook, who, it will be remembered, passed many months in New Zealand altogether, and the greater part of the time in the north. He discovered that kauri was superior to Norway pine, or indeed, to any other wood then known, for spars and topmasts of vessels. Other explorers endorsed his opinion of it, and in 1820 the British Government sent a ship, the *Dromedary*, to New Zealand, for the purpose of obtaining kauri timber. It was then classed high at Lloyd's.

Subsequently a demand for kauri timber arose in Sydney and elsewhere. Some trade in it was established with the Maoris; and little communities of English sawyers settled here and there along the coast of New Zealand. This was one among other causes that led to the colonization of the country in 1840. Thus the kauri holds a place in history,

* See *Pronunciation of Maori Names*, in the Appendix.

having had its share in making this our Brighter Britain.

The value of the kauri to New Zealand at large, and to the North in particular, can hardly be overrated. It is an important export, being sent to other parts of the colony, to Australia, the South Sea Islands, and elsewhere. In its own country it is used for every purpose to which timber is applicable. The many other trees of the bush are neglected for the sake of it; while it is more plentiful than any of them. Settlers in other parts of the colony, beyond the limit of the kauri's growth, make use of their native timbers, but lament that the cost of transport prevents them from importing kauri, so much superior is it. Wherever it is necessary to bring timber from a distance, as in comparatively treeless Otago for example, kauri is preferred; though it will have to be brought from further away than totara, miro, or matai, which are cut in southern forests.

One may say that the kauri is to Northern New Zealand what the oak has been to England, and even more. There, houses are built of it almost exclusively; it is used in the construction of vessels, for fencing, furniture, and all the more general purposes. And its valuable resin is the kauri gum of commerce; but that I must speak of separately.

Not alone is the kauri monarch in the forests of

New Zealand, but it must rank among the royallest trees the earth produces. It grows, for the most part, in forests sacred to itself, not mixing with the common herd of trees. In this respect other kinds of pine are similar. Also, each distinct tract of kauri bush, or forest, contains trees of a certain uniformity of age, consequently of size. In the aggregate vast tracts are covered with it. The largest forest of kauri is that between the Hokianga and the Kaipara waters, which, I believe, is to be put down at nearly a thousand square miles in extent, bush of a more varied description intervening here and there among it. After it come the kauri forests of Mongonui, Whangaroa, and Coromandel.

There are few experiences more impressive to the feelings than to stand alone in the recesses of a kauri forest. Unlike the character of the mixed bush—the forest where trees of many other kinds are found—the kauri bush is weirdly depressing from its terrible monotony. It is solemn, sombre, and gloomy to the last degree. Yet is there a profound majesty about it that awes one in spite of oneself.

The trees stand closely together, not branching out much till near the top. They cover range and gully, mountain and plain, in unbroken succession. At the base they may girth as much as up to fifty feet. Forty feet of girth is not uncommon, and thirty feet is often the average. They soar up straight to a hundred, a hundred and fifty, even to a hundred and eighty feet before branching, and then their leafy crowns, interlaced together, form a canopy through which daylight hardly penetrates.

The boles of these woodland giants are mostly black and smooth, sometimes covered with twigs, though this chiefly in the smaller trees. Supplejack, bush-lawyer, mounga, various creeper-ferns with magnificent fronds, and sometimes flowering clematis, swing from trunk to trunk and knit the columns together. Below there is not the thick undergrowth that prevails in the varied bush, but a lighter tangle of shrubs. Ferns, among which several varieties like the maidenhair predominate, grow waist-high in rank luxuriance.

The sublime grandeur of a kauri forest is hardly equalled by anything else of the kind in nature. One seems to stand amid the aisles of a mighty temple, shut out from the world and imprisoned amid endless ranks of tremendous columns. Stillness and silence deepen the profundity of gloom around one. The fiercest gale may be raging overhead, and not a leaf is stirred within the dark coverts; only the faint murmur of the foliage far above betrays what is passing. Of life there is nothing visible. The little fantails, the traveller's friends in the bush, hover around one, and they are all one sees, unless it be, perchance, the rapid flash of a rat running up some trunk, or the scuttling of a kiwi or weka amid the fern.

To get some real notion of what these forests are like let us compare them with English woods. The latter bear the palm of beauty, but the former that of grandeur from their very vastness. The largest wood in England is but the size of one dingle in a kauri forest, and is flat and tame contrasted with the hilly ruggedness of the land here. Again, measure the girth of English beeches, oaks, elms, and ashes. The oldest and best grown woods will not give you an average girth of ten feet. Trees girthing fifteen to twenty feet are rare and singular. What is this to the giant kauri?

If we look at height there is another difference. English trees are remarkable for their limbs and branches. Take these away, and the stick that remains seldom averages more than thirty or forty feet. If it reaches to sixty the tree is regarded as something extraordinary. But the splendid dome of foliage, the beautiful spread of boughs, which is the glory of English oak or chestnut, is forbidden to the kauri. Its magnificence resides solely in its stick, which is more like a factory chimney than anything else. You get an impression of immensity, you feel a veritable pigmy as you walk, mile after mile, among trees whose girth is thirty feet, and whose branches only begin a hundred and thirty feet from the ground; while, every now and then, you come upon some patriarch of fifty feet girth and a hundred and eighty feet, perhaps, of stick.

An assertion has been made, that if the present rate of consumption be kept up, some eighty years will see the end of the kauri forests. This may be true, but I do not think it is. I fancy that it is a calculation made in ignorance of the real extent of the kauri bush. Also, that no true idea was conceived of the enormous bulk of the trees, and the countless number of them to be found far back from the rivers, in the less accessible regions of the bush. I think I might say, with quite as much show of reason, that if the present rate of consumption were even doubled, as it doubtless will be, a century may elapse before economy in cutting kauri need be studied.

When working with parties of the Government Land Survey, I had good opportunities for getting some idea of the stupendous supplies of kauri timber. I once counted forty trees on a measured acre. Of these the smallest had a girth of twenty feet, with a stick of about eighty feet in height; the largest might be about double that. We estimated that these trees would yield a million feet of sawn timber. Of course that is an exceptional instance, but it must be remembered that there are hundreds of square miles of kauri bush in the aggregate.

The annual output of the saw-mills is reckoned to be sixty million feet of sawn kauri timber, the value of which may be roughly put at £300,000. Much of this is used up in the colony; but an increasing export trade, amounting in value to £40,000 or £50,000 per annum, is carried on with Australia, Fiji, and the South Sea Islands. There are some twenty large saw-mills in various parts of the kauri forests, and there are other small ones which supply local demands; together these employ a large number of hands.

The largest mill is that at Te Kopura, on the Wairoa river, some forty-five miles above its outfall into the Kaipara harbour. It can turn out 120,000 feet per week. At Aratapu, higher up the same river, there is another mill, turning out 80,000 feet per week. These mills are working on the outskirts of the great Kaipara-Hokianga forest. Vessels drawing seventeen feet of water can come up the Wairoa to load at them. The mill at Whangaroa, on the east coast, ranks next in point of size, turning out sawn timber to the average annual value of

£23,000. At Whangapoua, in Coromandel, are two mills, cutting about 160,000 feet per week between them. The cost of their plant was £25,000. The Whangapoua kauri bush extends over some 30,000 acres.

Sawn kauri is sold at the mills at 9s. 6d. to 11s. 6d. per hundred feet. The high freights cause it to cost 15s. to 17s. in the southern ports, and, I believe, it is sold at about the same in Sydney or the Islands. It would not be easy to say what is the average yield of a tree, the difference being very considerable. Some put it down at 10,000 feet, but I am sure that is an under estimate.

A stick of fifty feet length, and thirty feet in circumference at the base, might be reckoned to yield about 20,000 feet of sawn timber. The value of this would be £100. Deducting £40 as the cost of felling, transporting to the mill, and cutting up, a profit of £60 is left. This is a fair example. When a stick of a hundred and fifty feet, with a girth of forty or fifty feet, is in question, both work and profit are larger, of course.

The stump of one of these titanic trees is no small affair. It is big enough to build a small house upon, if sawn flat. I remember once making one of a party of eight, and dancing a quadrille on the stump of a kauri.

There is a variety of the tree known as the mottled kauri. The wood of this is very curious and beautiful, and fetches a high price for cabinet work. It is not very common, and when a big tree of this kind is come upon, it is a source of great gratification to its owner, for it may yield him £500 or £600 of absolute profit.

Felling big trees with the axe is tremendous labour. Till recently it was the only means employed here. Perhaps you may have to cut five or six feet deep into the tree, in order to reach the heart of it. To do this an enormous gash must be made, so large in fact, that scaffoldings have to be erected within it, to permit the workmen to reach their mark. Only two men can cut at the same gash at a time; but frequent shifts are resorted to, so as to "keep the pot boiling." Now, a saw working between portable engines is more generally employed upon the big trees.

When the great stick has been laid prostrate, with a crash that resounds for miles, and a shock that makes the whole hillside quiver, it is cut into lengths, and roughly squared with long-handled axes. Then comes the process of getting it to the mill, which may possibly be a considerable distance off.

The hilly and rugged character of the land nearly

always prevents anything like a tramway system being adopted; and, for a long time, trees were only cut where they could be readily run down into the water. But a system has been introduced, by an American bushman, I believe, which is now generally used, and by means of which the largest trees can be got out anywhere in this country of heights and hollows.

The logs are easily collected in the bottom of the nearest gully, as they can be readily sent down the sides of the ranges by means of screw-jacks, rollers and slides. When the sides of the gully have been denuded of their timber, and a huge collection of logs lies piled in the bottom, preparation is made to further their descent to the river. A dam is built right across the ravine below the logs, constructed of timber, earth, stones, and whatever material comes handiest.

When the winter rains commence, the first day or two of continued downpour causes every little water-course to swell into a foaming torrent. The stream in the gully pours down a great volume of water, which, checked by the dam, spreads out behind it into a broad lake that fills all the lower ground. In this flood the mighty logs are borne up, and float upon its surface.

The sides of the dam, which is angularly shaped,

are chiefly supported by logs set up endways as buttresses upon the lower side. To these supports ropes are attached, which are carried up the hillsides out of reach of the water, above the level of the swollen flood pent in by the dam. Then men and horses, or bullocks, haul with sudden and united effort upon the ropes; the chief supports are torn away; the dam breaks down in various places; the waters overflow and stream through the breaches. Or, sometimes, the dam is flushed by breaching it with gunpowder or dynamite. Soon the mass of water moves with irresistible force, breaking down what is left of the dam and sweeping everything before it. Then, in mighty volume, it rushes down the gully, bearing onward with it the great collection of massive logs that it has floated. Sometimes the first flush carries the timber down to the open river. Sometimes the entire process has to be repeated more than once or twice, if the distance be long, or the nature of the ground necessitate it.

When they fall into the river, or inlet of the sea, as the case may be, the logs are brought up by booms ready to receive them. They are then chained together in rafts and floated down to the mill, which, of course, gives upon the water-highway. Often such a flush will constitute a whole year's work, or longer; and will provide a supply of raw material for the saw-mill that will last it as long. But exactly the same process may be practically and profitably carried out for only a few logs, where the gully is not large, and not too far from the river.

Our own special little community are pioneer farmers, of course, and we do not employ ourselves in this way. Still, some of us have in former years acted the part of lumberers, or bushmen proper, when we were working at any jobs that turned up. The work we have is heavy enough in all conscience, but it is light compared to the tremendous labour that bushmen have to get through.

The lowest rate of wages for bushmen is 25*s*. per week, and all found. But the rate varies, better men getting better wages, the paucity of hands affecting the scale, and strikes for more pay occurring sometimes. I have known the hands of a saw-mill to get as much as seven or nine shillings per day.

Usually there are comfortable barracks for the men employed at a mill; but, when working up in the bush, these are not always available, and the workmen are lodged in huts, or shanties, upon the ground, being in much the same case as we are in our shanty. Their employers supply them with all necessaries, and have to be pretty careful in this respect, as your bushman will not work unless he gets tucker according to a very liberal scale. Beef, mutton and pork, bread, potatoes, kumera and tea he gets in unlimited quantities, besides various other items that need not be catalogued.

Most of our produce is taken by the saw-mills at the market-price. We have even sent them our fat steers and wethers, instead of shipping them to Auckland; and one year we made a good thing by growing cabbages and fresh vegetables for the bushmen. Like English colliers, they look to have the best food going; and, what is more, they get it. Yet it must be remembered that the bushman's work is terribly hard. It needs the employment of all the physical strength and vigour a man has to bestow, and this must be used with a continued pertinacity that is excessively trying.

Kauri-gum—or Kapia, as the Maoris call it—which has been just alluded to, is another peculiar product of this northern extremity of New Zealand. It is not of any practical service to the colonists, as the timber of the tree which produces it is, but it is an export of considerably greater value. It is the solidified sap, or resin of the kauri, but not in a fresh form; it is that resin in a hardened condition found buried in the ground.

There are tracts of country, known as gum-fields, in which the kauri-gum is to be dug up most plentifully. These places are stretches of bleak moorland for the most part, though not invariably. The soil in them consists very much of a heavy yellow clay, loose and friable near the surface. It is impregnated with fragments and particles of gum, which may be found in numerous spots to occur in layers and collections of larger pieces, varying in size up to blocks the size of a man's body. It is not usual to collect pieces smaller than the closed fist— minuter fragments not being considered remunerative to the digger.

The gum is found just below the surface of the ground, and sometimes down to the depth of six or eight feet. The finding of it, collecting and bringing to market, affords a sufficiently profitable occupation to have constituted a distinct class of men, who go by the name of gum-diggers.

Gum-fields are poor lands usually, though some are adapted for settlement. The country lying between Riverhead, Helensville, and Ararimu, which I described when relating our journey up-country, is a fair example of a gum-field. But gum is also found in the kauri forests, round the roots of the trees, especially of old, partly decayed, or wholly dead specimens. It is also to be found pretty generally throughout all the land of the kauri. Of course it cannot be discovered everywhere, or in all soils, but traces of it will be apparent somewhere in any single square mile; and in every sort of land throughout the limit of the kauri's growth, gum will be found here and there. Thus, on our farm and in the surrounding bush, although these are distinctly not gum-lands, there are little patches of ground, of a few acres in extent, whence we have got a ton or two of gum at times.

It is worthy of remark that the fresh resin of the living trees is not of any commercial value. Great masses of gum are often found in forks and clefts of the trees, and about the roots; but of this, only a little of the latter is generally worth anything, the rest being soft and in a condition that renders it valueless. It seems that the gum must be buried underground for a considerable time, an unknown term of years, before it attains the degree of hardness and other qualities that merchants require.

I have been told that the Maoris collect the soft, fresh gum and bury it, so that they or their descendants may dig it up again after sufficient time has elapsed for it to undergo the requisite changes. Whether this is so or not I am unable to say of my personal knowledge. I have never met with any instance of the kind, and have strong doubts as to the forecasting care with which such a tale credits the Maoris. They are certainly not given to providing for a distant future in a general way.

OUR SPECIAL PRODUCTS.

It would seem that the deposits of gum in the soil are all that remains of ancient kauri forests. These must once have covered the open fern-lands, where no trace of them now remains, except rich gum-holes here and there. It would seem that the kauri had, in the course of ages, exhausted the soil on which they grew, of constituents necessary to their growth, and had then naturally died out in such localities. The existing forests are, of course, making new deposits, which will some day be available. Felling the trees necessarily causes a diminution of this, but possibly some means may yet be discovered of rendering the fresh, soft gum equally useful with the semi-fossil kind.

Kauri-gum is very like amber in general appearance, and is similar to it in chemical characteristics; but it is much more brittle, and hence is not of such value for ornaments. Many colonists amuse themselves with carving and polishing trinkets of gum, but they chip too readily to permit of their ever being of value. Kauri-gum has sometimes been fraudulently substituted for amber, but the better specimens of the latter have a yellow tint which is seldom seen in the New Zealand product. Our gum exists of various shades of brown and sherry-colour, both clear and clouded. The most highly-prized variety is colourless like glass, or nearly so, and some is found almost black, not unlike jet. Flies, fragments of moss, and so on, are occasionally seen embedded in it.

Kauri-gum was first brought into notice at the time of the first colonization, in 1840 and 1841. It was then collected chiefly by Maoris, and was sold by them to the store-keepers. Its value at that time was only £5 or £6 per ton; and about a hundred tons was all the annual export for some years.

Since then, however, an increasing demand for it arose in the United States. New York and Boston now take two-thirds of all the gum exported; and of what is sent home to England the greater part is re-shipped thence to American ports. The number of gum-diggers regularly employed is supposed to have exceeded four thousand at times; now they average some two thousand altogether. The amount of the export steadily increased from the first, until, in 1870-71-72, it reached to some fifteen thousand tons for the three years, valued at half a million sterling.

Subsequent to this there was very considerable falling off in the export. The number of diggers decreased, fields were declared worked out, and it was thought that the supplies were exhausted. But after a year or two, it was discovered that gum existed in many places where its presence had been hitherto unsuspected; and it was also made clear that large deposits were often underlying the two or three feet of surface-soil previously worked, on the fields it was thought were exhausted.

A fresh impulse was given to gum-digging, and the amount of the export rose again. In 1878, it stood at 3410 tons; in 1879, at 3247 tons; in 1880, as much as 5500 was shipped, valued at £236,500. From 1853 to 1880 inclusive, about 70,000 tons were sent out, export value £2,100,000. It would thus seem that kauri-gum is more plentiful now than ever, while its average value has risen to £43 per ton.

Some American scientist has given it as his opinion that the kauri-gum exported from 1840 to 1880 must have required a forest-growth of ten thousand years to have produced it; but then we know that scientists will go making these rash assertions on the very vaguest premises. How long ago the kauri forests that covered the now open fern-lands died out, it would be hard to say. And how long they had stood before that is an equally difficult problem to solve. Of the trees in the forests now standing we can easily calculate the age. Some of them were already big trees at the period when Julius Cæsar was colonizing the other Britain. Doubtless the forests here were pretty much what they are to-day, when Norman and Saxon and Dane were fighting for the throne.

Gum-diggers receive an all-round price for the gum they bring down to the stores, which fluctuates somewhat in amount. It usually averages about £30 a ton. Before reaching its final market, the gum is cleaned, picked, and carefully assorted and re-assorted into six or eight different classes. The very best of these has been known to sell at £144 per ton in New York; the others at varying prices down to £25 or £20 for the lowest class. The average price is now £43 per ton.

The use to which kauri-gum is put is the manufacture of varnish. At least this is the general theory. It is made into a varnish much resembling that of copal; and gum copal, as the reader will remember, is the product of the *Hymenea verrucosa* of tropical Eastern Africa, where it is dug from the ground much as kauri-gum is here.

Varnish-making is the assigned use of kauri-gum, but there is a dark suspicion afloat in our Brighter Britain that this is not the only nor the chief one. It is hinted that the Yankees use it to adulterate something or other with, or to fix up some compound of a wholly different kind. I will not say that O'Gaygun is solely responsible for this insinuation, but he certainly fosters it in every way he can.

In the mind of our Milesian ally there exists a profound belief that the principal object in life of an American is to invent new and profitable ways of adulteration, or to discover means of perfecting colossal shams, and thereby defrauding a guileless public, such as ourselves.

For my own part, I disagree with O'Gaygun on this point. Experience has led me to believe that the English manufacturer and trader stand unrivalled in all the arts of adulteration. The Yankee is a babe compared to them at this game. In fact, so far as exports are concerned, it would seem as if the British merchant could not help a greater or lesser measure of chicanery. What the Yankee sends to us is generally good; this in other matters besides hardware.

But O'Gaygun's views are warped, and his conclusions are mainly drawn from the remembrance of one incident, the tale of which he is never weary of narrating.

It seems that, shortly before he came out to New Zealand, O'Gaygun was concerned with others in the exportation from Ireland to America of a certain mineral. It was a heavy, white, glistening earth, which I take to have been witherite, or carbonate of baryta.

This stuff was sold ostensibly for paint-making,

and certain Yankee merchants bought up all they could of it. Shipload after shipload went to America, and the Irish speculators were in high glee as the demand for it increased; although such a quantity had been shipped as would have sufficed to have whitewashed the entire two continents.

At last the real destination of the mineral came to light. It was powdered and mixed with flour, which America was then exporting largely to Europe. It made the finest flours heavier, and made seconds rank as first-class. So, according to O'Gaygun, hundreds and thousands of tons of this witherite were eaten by cheated Europe in the form of bread. A whole mountain, so he says, was shipped to the land of the Stars and Stripes; and as much as was sent came back to Europe as flour.

When the thing was blown upon, of course, the export gradually ceased. And I believe that O'Gaygun and his associates were blamed for participation in the fraud. Therefore he, poor, deluded Irishman, has ever since held the Yankee to be of very nature iniquitous in all his dealings. Well, let us hope that kauri-gum is, after all, only an innocent varnish basis, as is generally stated, and that it is not eaten as pork or beans or anything by a too-confiding British public.

The gum-diggers of Northern New Zealand are

a peculiar body of nomads. They are recruited from every nation, and from every rank of society, and, like the communities gathered together on Australian or Californian gold-fields, present a strange medley of opposites.

Among them one may come across men who are graduates of the universities. One may find members of noble houses, representatives of historic names; nay, twice I have met men born to titles gum-digging. Then one may find diggers who should belong to professions they have abandoned— civil, military, learned, artistic. Clerks, accountants, secretaries, and shopmen swell the ranks of our Bohemian army. There are guileless peasants, natives of Norfolk or Devon, France or Germany, perhaps; and there are runaway sailors, ex-convicts, tinkers, tailors, printers' devils, pirates, rowdies, negroes, Kanakas, Maoris, Chinamen; a collection of gentlemen educated to every pursuit under the sun, in fact.

Throughout all this heterogeneous assemblage there exists entire equality, but little fraternization. Each man is as good as his fellow; there is no recognized line of demarcation between man and man. Yet gum-diggers are not gregarious as a rule; they are too jealous, each of another's possible luck, to admit of general brotherhood. Generally little gangs associate together and work in company; but it is rare that they do so on communistic principles. More often, each member of the gang works entirely for his own hand, though they may have food and so on in common.

There is precious little feeling of *caste*, or prejudice on account of different social ranks, remaining to us in this free land. What there is, however, places gum-diggers, as a class, on the bottommost level of society. Not that even that distinction conveys any slight upon individual gum-diggers; it is more a sort of abstract principle, than anything real or practical.

Still, they are sneered at occasionally by other colonists. It is a favourite theory that, if you should see some particularly haughty swell come out with all the pomp of a first-class passage, some grandiose creature of the scapegrace-fine-gentleman sort, with such airs and dignity as befit a man who feels that the colony was made for him, and not he for the colony, you may chuckle over his probable descent to gum-digging very soon. You have to get out of his lordly path while the air of the quarter-deck is round him, feeling that this humble country is only too much honoured by his mere presence in it. But, in a few months' time, you come across him on the gum-field, in ankle-jacks and ragged shirt, picking up a scanty living. He is Captain Gorgeous Dashabout no longer.

There is a certain charm about gum-digging, particularly to people of unsettled and gypsy-like disposition. You have no boss. You can do as you like; work when you like, and how you like; and lie on your back when it pleases you to do so, without fear of being rowed at by any one. Moreover, with ordinary luck, you can make as good wages as by working on a farm, and that with less actual toil, though possibly some additional hardship.

Gum-diggers must be equipped as lightly as possible. It is commonly said that a blanket, a spade, a gum-spear, a knife, a hatchet, a billy, a pipe, some provisions and tobacco, together with the clothes he stands in, constitute all that a gum-digger needs in the way of outfit. He really cannot afford to possess much more, for he must hump all his belongings on his own back, over mountain and dale, forest and morass. This is one reason why small parties associate together, besides for company. They can then manage to carry a better sufficiency of things with them from camp to camp.

Where proximity to a settlement, a road, or a river permits of it, it is possible for gum-diggers to make their camps pretty comfortable. Often it is not necessary to move camp for months at a time, when the surrounding field is pretty rich in gum-holes. But they are not a provident class, seldom caring for anything beyond the present moment.

The occupation is simplicity itself. Once the prospecting has been accomplished and the district determined on, the party move to it as best they can. Nearly always there is a long tramp through the wilds, with the necessaries on back and shoulders. Then a camp is formed in some favourable spot near a stream; a rude hut is constructed of such material as is at hand; and a store of firewood is cut.

For work, each man straggles about all day by himself, with his spear and spade and sack. He tries every likely looking place with the spear, which is simply an iron rod, sharp at one end, and with a wooden handle at the other. When the end of the spear touches buried gum, there is a peculiar clip or "feel," which the digger knows. Then he digs out the gum, fills his sack, and carries it to camp, continuing to work the same spot as long as it yields anything, when he goes on to look for another. In the evenings he scrapes and cleans the day's take with his knife.

Sometimes a digger will not get a shilling's worth of gum in a whole week's work; sometimes he will find five or six pounds' worth in an hour. Generally speaking, and taking one week with another, he may earn £2 to £4 a week. When enough has been collected and scraped it is carried down to the nearest bush-store or settlement, where it is at once sold. Provisions are bought, and the surplus may be banked, though, in nine cases out of ten, it goes in a "lush up." Some gum-diggers save till they can get down to Auckland, and then they have a high old time of it as long as the money lasts.

It will be seen how this kind of life appeals to the ne'er-do-well. Luck and chance are elements in it; and it is a free, roving, devil-may-care existence. Hence it is that scapegraces take to it so kindly, and prefer its risks and manifest hardships to the steady work of farm-labourers or bushmen.

Gum-diggers seldom make much money. They get a living, and that is about all. Now and then they may do better, but it only results in a "burst." Yet gum-digging has often been a great assistance to settlers. We have taken to it at times, in order to raise a little ready money, when the farm was not paying. Many a small, needy settler has found it a resource to stave off ruin. To energetic and industrious men it offers good wages on the whole, and, as a temporary thing, many such have taken advantage of it.

There are even men among the regular gum-diggers who are superior to their class. These may save all they make, till they have enough to start a small pioneer-farm, or to set up in some handicraft. Thus, in spite of the acknowledged evil repute of the gum-digger, there will be and are, in our Brighter Britain, comfortable homes, whose proprietors will tell you that they are founded and built upon kauri-gum, so to speak.

CHAPTER II.

OUR CLASSIC GROUND.

WHEN the history of New Zealand comes to be written, and when a new generation finds time to look back upon the country's past, that also having grown with the coming years, a new want will imperceptibly arise. A desire will develop in people's minds for something to reverence. Out of the crudest materials will be erected monuments to the past, and the older these become the more they will be esteemed, while the events they speak of will come to be regarded as of greater and greater importance. So it has been with England; so it has been in America; so it will be in Australia and New Zealand. Nay, already the first symptoms of the feeling are beginning to appear among us.

America has gathered all the force of sacred memories round Plymouth Rock and Bunker Hill, Manhattan and Yorktown, and other places commemorative of the crises, or romantic episodes, of her history. So, in like manner, shall our descendants find spots connected with the long ago, whose tales shall serve to quicken the glow of patriotic sentiment in their hearts.

Laugh, reader, if you like. The early events of our history seem so trivial to you now. You cannot get up any enthusiasm about them, anyhow. Yet future generations will have another and more generous feeling. A time will come when crowds of tourists, guide-book in hand, will rush from southern cities to "do" those quiet places that now seem utterly forgotten. Take my word for it; that of a man who never romanced!

Probably there will be spots of more or less renown scattered up and down throughout all the country. But the region destined to be most widely known and justly celebrated, held in high regard from its wealth of associations with the earliest days of our history, and esteemed not lightly either for its natural scenery, is that comprised within the three counties of Bay of Islands, Mongonui, and Hokianga. Already, even, this is worthy to be named the classic ground of New Zealand.

Some of our little community in the Kaipara go up into the Bay not infrequently. We have good friends living up in that part, and we go on pleasure as well as on business. Dandy Jack is up there oftenest of any, for he does some trade in those districts in horses and cattle. One or two of us go to help him, and we have, on certain occasions, joined land-surveying expeditions, whose head-quarters were in the Bay. So that, on the whole, we know the three counties tolerably well.

Our route from here lies through the Maungaturoto bush, and up to Mangapai and Whangarei, a distance of forty-and-odd miles. Beyond that is another stretch of about the same distance, before the Kawakawa is reached. The greater part of the way lies through dense forest, but there is a track along which it is possible to ride. This is called a road in these parts, but as the most experienced bushman is apt to lose it altogether on occasions, its actual character may be guessed. I believe Dandy Jack did once accomplish the whole journey to the Kawakawa in two days. As a rule, however, it takes us four. The nature of the track is not adapted for quick riding, so that twenty or twenty-five miles is about as much as we can make in the day.

We have to camp out at nights, of course, except the one night we put up at Whangarei, but this is no uncommon experience for us. There are some creeks to be crossed that are rather ugly when full of water; one or two must be swum sometimes. It is a fearful and arduous job to bring cattle along this road, as might be expected. Some are pretty sure to be lost out of the drove, while some will get stuck in the mud of marshes and crossings, and a rare job it is to extricate them.

Once we had a pack-horse with us, laden with stores and utensils for a surveyor's camp. He was led with a rope as we rode. Just at one of the worst parts he broke away and bolted, kicking and bucking as he went, the result being that the baggage went flying in all directions. It took us half a day or more to recapture the horse, and to pick up his scattered load. This will serve to illustrate some of the pleasing incidents of travel in the bush.

On one occasion Old Colonial, Dandy Jack, and I were camped somewhere beyond Whangarei. We were making the journey up to fetch down some cattle. We were in a little dingle beside a small stream. The huge fire was blazing merrily in front, lighting up the tree-trunks with weird effect, and making the shadows of the forest round us seem more profound. Near by our horses were tethered, and we lay, now our supper was done, rolled in our blankets, pipes in mouth, and heads pillowed on our saddles.

We were talking of some improvements that had been recently effected in the settlements, and from that we got to speculating on the future. Dandy

Jack was wearily sighing for the good time when there should be a decent road constructed along this route.

"Wonder whether I shall live to see it;" he said.

"Of course you will," replied Old Colonial, who is nothing if not optimistic in his views.

"I tell you what; we shall all live to see not only a good road through this, but farms and settlements and hotels along it!"

"Bravo!" returned Dandy Jack. "Then I'll start a coach to run from Kawa-kawa to Whangarei, and on to Mangawai, or across to Te Pahi, perhaps. Might pick up some trade, don't you think?"

"I reckon your coach would be a failure, old man," continued Old Colonial. "I expect to see a railway one of these days, connecting Auckland with the Bay, and all the places between. Not much room for your coach then!"

"Oh, they'll not make a railroad up here this century."

"I expect they will, though," said our chief, impressively.

"And, look here! I'll tell you what's going to help make business for it. The Bay and Hokianga are our classic ground."

"Classic ground?"

"Certainly. Here are the places where Captain

Cook came, and Tasman, and all the early voyagers. Here's where the first missionaries came; where colonization commenced; where British sovereignty was established. Here's where the history of the early days has got to be written. Here's where Hongi lived, and Hone Heke after him; where the first Maori war was fought; where battles were won, and pas stormed, and treaties signed. This is the most illustrious district in the whole colony. Whatever memories we've got date from here. I tell you that streams of tourists will want to come and see these places some day. We ought to make more of them now than we do."

So rhapsodized Old Colonial, after a manner that occasionally affects him, while the forest gleamed redly round us with the reflection of our camp-fire, and a bittern boomed in mockery and remonstrance from a neighbouring swamp. I heard Dandy Jack softly murmuring to the trees—

> "Meet nurse for a poetic child;
> Land of brown heath and shaggy wood!
> Land of the mountain and the flood!"

And when Old Colonial attempted to continue—

"If this isn't classic ground, what is, I should like to know? Posterity will——"

Dandy Jack cut him short with a loud declamation from "Locksley Hall." But I remembered the allusion to classic ground, in spite of our merriment at the time, and, accordingly, it finds effect in this chapter.

The little settlement of Mangapai is much like those we are accustomed to in the Kaipara. It is situated on a creek and inlet of the Whangarei Harbour. But the township of Whangarei itself, some eight miles further north, is in a considerably more advanced stage than anything we can show.

The harbour is something like our Kaipara, only of less extent. It is a considerable inlet of the sea, with Heads at the entrance, some tidal rivers, and creeks navigable for a short distance. There is direct communication by sea with Auckland, kept up by means of sundry schooners and sailing-craft. The large steamer *Iona*, which plies between Auckland, Bay of Islands, and Mongonui every week, calls at Whangarei Heads on each trip for passengers. A small steamer plies within the harbour itself.

Whangarei township is a remarkably favourable specimen of a bush settlement. It stands on a river, and is about seventeen miles distant from the Heads. The little town occupies a flat, rendered very picturesque by the gardens about the houses, and by a surrounding amphitheatre of bush-clothed heights. There is a church, hotels, stores, schools, mills, streets and roads, even a local newspaper, to bear evidence to the energy and prosperity of the settlers.

The district round about the Whangarei waters is rich soil for the most part, mainly covered with bush in its natural condition. Settlement took place here a good many years before it was begun in the Kaipara, consequently more improvement has been effected. The pioneer farms and homesteads show a surprising amount of comfort. They have lots of grass for pasturage, and two or three thousand acres of plough-lands in the aggregate as well.

Then there are two special industries in the place. One is lime-burning, the product being sent to supply Auckland demands for it. The other is coal-mining. A mine was opened here some years ago, and was afterwards flooded and consequently closed, remaining unworked for some time. It has now again been re-opened, and is in full swing of work, though the operations are only carried out in a small way comparatively.

One would think that the road, so called, connecting two settlements of such relative importance as Whangarei and Kawa-kawa, would be a better one than it is. The distance is between forty and fifty miles, and there is no settlement between. The road is just a track, along which it is possible to ride and drive cattle. A good part of the way lies through heavy bush.

But there is really very little traffic between these places, and what there is can be best transacted by sea. It is the general fashion in a country like this. Each settlement requires water-communication with Auckland, and cares little at present for anything else. A settler makes a road down to the river, or to the settlement on the river, sufficient for his own purposes, and as short as possible. That is all he particularly wants. The necessity for roads between settlements, and to open up the back-country, only grows gradually with time. Of course in other parts of the colony, where there is not water everywhere as in the North, the case is widely different. A good road or a railway is the first and chief thing needed there.

At Kawa-kawa we are in the Bay of Islands, and consequently within the classic ground. Indeed, south-east of Kawa-kawa is the site of the famous pa of Ruapekapeka, which was a strong native fortress, constructed with a degree of skill, and science almost, that astonished military engineers.

The Kawa-kawa river gives its name to the district. There is a good deal of settlement and pioneer-farming round here and in Pakaru district, but the chief industry of the place is coal-mining.

A hundred to a hundred and fifty colliery hands are employed, forming, with their families, a good nucleus of population. Manganese and cement are also mined here.

The seam is twelve and a half feet thick; and the output about three thousand tons a month. There are some half-dozen miles of railway, connecting the mine with a suitable shipping-place, near where the river joins the waters of the bay itself. A fleet of coasters is constantly employed carrying coal to Grahamstown and Auckland. Extensive coal-beds exist in many parts of the North, but Whangarei and Kawa-kawa are the only workings at present. I have seen some carbonized cocoa-nuts extracted from the Kawa-kawa mine, which prove that the cocoa-nut palm must once have grown here, though it does not now.

There is nothing particularly classic about a colliery village, however, although it may be situated in a primeval solitude, and amid woodland scenery, where axe and spade are busy converting the wilds into cultivated farms. The river winds down through grand mountainous tracts, and then we find ourselves on the bosom of the gloriously beautiful bay, the most picturesque and most romantic of all places in the North—more, the home of the first chapters of our history.

I will not go so far as to say that the Bay of Islands is as lovely as Sydney Harbour, nor can I allow that it throws certain choice bits of scenery in the Kaipara and the Hokianga estuaries entirely into the shade. But it certainly is a most picturesque place. The views are so varied, so wholly unique; and the stories connected with every corner of the bay throw such a romantic halo over the whole, that I feel quite justified in endorsing the opinion that the Bay of Islands is, and always must be, the most remarkable place in Northern New Zealand.

The entrance of the bay is guarded by two great rocky headlands, Cape Wiwiki and Cape Brett. These stand some twelve miles apart, and the distance from them to the back of the bay is about twenty miles. But numerous inlets open up into the land, and four considerable creeks, the Keri-keri, Waitangi, Kawa-kawa, and Waitari fall into the bay, forming large estuaries at their junction with it. The promontories, headlands, and indentations of the shores, together with the hundred islands and islets that thickly stud the waters, diversify the scenery very much, and cause you to think, as you sail or row between them, that you are gliding from river into river and from channel into channel, with broad lake-like reaches interspersed.

About fifteen miles from Cape Brett, and on the same side of the bay, a promontory of considerable size juts out. Upon the inner side of this stands Kororareka, capital of the Bay, and its port of entry.

Officialism has recently been trying very hard to alter the name of this place into Russell, which action is much deprecated by settlers, who insist upon retaining the old native name. The reason for the proposed change is not very clear, and why this particular town should have been so singled out is equally inexplicable to the unofficial mind. It seems to be a great pity, in any case, to bestow such names as Smithville, or Russell, or New London upon growing settlements, the future cities of a future nation. It is a pity because they are not distinctive, nor expressive of the country upon which they are grafted. How much better to retain the old native names, which carry with them sound and meaning both original and peculiar. Educated Americans are beginning to find this out, and to regret the loss of an indigenous character, which springs from the vulgarity and confusion of their nomenclature. How much better are such names as Pensacola or Tallahassee, than New Orleans or New York?

In New Zealand native names have been very

largely retained, though less so in the south than in the north. But jacks in office are for ever trying to perpetuate their own names, or those of individuals whom they toady, by making them do duty for towns or counties or rivers. It is a "vulgarian atrocity," similar to that which moves a cockney soul to scratch its ignoble appellative upon pyramid or monolith.

In this particular instance, it is a positive shame to hurl such an insulting degradation into our classic ground. Kororareka, under that name, is the oldest settlement in the colony. It is intimately associated with early history. Kororareka—"The Beach of Shells"—was once a native kainga. Then it became a whaling station, and earned notoriety as a piratical stronghold, and the pandemonium of the Pacific. From that it was erected into the first capital of the colony, metropolis and seat of government for all New Zealand, under Mr. Busby, the British resident, and, in 1840, Captain Hobson, the first governor. It was plundered and burnt by Heke and Kawiti, and was a central point of the first Maori war.

Kororareka is a quiet little village now, and is never likely to grow into much more, unless it should become a manufacturing centre. Other places must take the trade of the district eventually. Hence,

Kororareka will always rest its chief claim to note upon its past history; so to call it Russell is to spoil its little romance. It is an outrageous vandalism, a nonsensical piece of spite or idiotcy that, in a philological and sentimental sense, is almost to be regarded as a crime.

As you come into sight of Kororareka from the bay, you are favourably impressed by its appearance. The town stands upon a wide flat, bordered by a high beach of white shingle and shells, from the centre of which a large wharf runs out for shipping to come alongside. A street of houses, stores and hotels principally, faces the beach, and gives the place all the airs of a miniature Brighton or Margate. Some other straggling streets run back from this.

The background is a low grassy range, evidently farm-lands. This range shuts out all view of the bay on the other side of the promontory. To the right it merges into the mountain tract that sentinels the Waitari and Kawa-kawa estuaries. On the left rises an abrupt and wooded hill, fissured with many romantic little glens and hollows. From this eminence, to which a road winds up from the town through the woods, a most magnificent view is obtainable. A great part of the panorama of this island-studded harbour lies stretched below one's feet; and on the highest crest is a certain famous flagstaff.

OUR CLASSIC GROUND.   43

Kororareka is not very large. The resident population is probably not more than two or three hundred. Farming industry round it is comparatively small. Its communication overland with other places is not good, and the hilly character of the contiguous land presents great difficulties in the way of the formation of roads. The place depends on its harbour, which is much used by whalers, who come here to tranship or sell oil, and to take in supplies. Quiet and dead-alive as it seems in general, there are times when a number of vessels are assembled here, and when bustle and business is consequently pretty brisk.

Before settled government and colonization overtook New Zealand, this spot had achieved an unsavoury reputation. Originally a native town, it had gradually become the resort of whaling-ships. Traders established themselves here, and a rowdy population of runaway sailors, ex-convicts, bad characters, and debauched Maoris filled the place. Drunkenness and riot were the general order of things; and it was even said that Kororareka was developing into a nest of pirates. There was no sort of government to restrain the evil, and man's passions, as usual, were transforming a natural Eden into a moral hell.

During these days of anarchy there is no doubt

that Kororareka was a sad thorn in the side to the missionaries, who were achieving wonderful results among the native tribes. The wanton profligacy of whites in Kororareka infected their converts, and interfered sadly with the Christianizing of the Maoris. Moreover, other places of a like nature began to spring up here and there on the coasts.

One would have thought that sober, God-fearing men would have hailed the establishment of British government, and would have done much to further colonization. Such, however, was far from being the idea or action of the early missionaries. So far as the missionaries in New Zealand were themselves concerned, they would seem to have turned a very cold shoulder to such of their countrymen as adventured thither, independently of the missions. So we are informed by one or two travellers who visited the country between 1814 and 1840. Nor is this feeling at all to be wondered at, considering the class of men who came to Kororareka. The European adventurers who came to New Zealand then were so generally of a loose and lawless order, that it is scarcely matter for surprise that missionaries should have looked askance at every white man they saw.

This feeling spread to the Societies at home in England, and was, doubtless, much exaggerated among their more zealous, but less large-minded supporters. It became mingled with a desire to preserve New Zealand for its aboriginal race ; to convert and civilize that people ; and to foster their self-government under the direct influence of the missionaries. And it must be borne in mind that the missionaries were really unacquainted with the extent of the country, and with the actual number of its native inhabitants ; while people in England had very vague ideas regarding their antipodes.

A party was formed in England, which has been styled "the Exeter Hall party." The persons adhering to its views did all in their power to prevent English colonization, or English government being established in New Zealand. The merits of the question as between them and their opponents need not concern us now.

The existence of such a place as Kororareka was felt to be a curse to the whole of the South Sea, and did not fail to affect even Sydney, two thousand miles away. There were not wanting some to press upon the Imperial Government the necessity of annexation and of active steps being taken. The Exeter Hall party, however, frustrated their endeavours, actuated thereto by motives that time has shown to have been founded on miscomprehension and mistake.

Guided by the Exeter Hall influence, and by representations made by the missionaries, the Imperial Government took a decided step in 1835. They recognized New Zealand as independent, treated with a confederation of Maori chiefs, and bestowed a national flag upon the country, thus forfeiting the claim acquired from Captain Cook's original discovery. Mr. Busby was appointed to be British resident at Kororareka ; as, however, he had no force to act with, he was unable to preserve order in that place, and he had neither influence nor power wherewith to uphold the dignity of his office and of the country he represented.

Persons in England who had been desirous of seeing New Zealand converted into an appanage of the British crown, covered their disappointment by forming an association, styled " The New Zealand Company," much upon the basis of the old East Indian Company. They proceeded to form settlements upon a system of their own; a pioneering expedition being sent out in 1839, and the first body of emigrants landing at Port Nicholson in 1840. Their action, together with the outcry caused by the condition of things at Kororareka, caused the Imperial Government to reverse its former policy.

Another circumstance operated to hasten the Government's decision. French Roman Catholic missions had been established in New Zealand, and were gaining many converts among the Maoris. In 1837 a French nobleman, one Baron de Thierry, purchased a large area in Hokianga, and sought to establish himself there as a sovereign prince. Then the French Government prepared to annex the islands as a possession of France.

In January, 1840, Captain Hobson arrived at Kororareka in command of H.M.S *Rattlesnake*, instructed to hoist the British standard, which he only succeeded in doing a few hours before a French ship arrived for a similar purpose. Captain Hobson at once found a staunch ally in the person of Tamati Waka, a powerful Ngapuhi chief. By this man's influence the Christianized chiefs of the North were gathered together, and induced to sign the famous Treaty of Waitangi, on March 5, 1840. That instrument is the title-deed of the colony. It was the formal cession of sovereignty to Queen Victoria, by the principal men of the Maori nation.

The missionaries have been severely criticized for the policy and line of action adopted by them, and by the Exeter Hall party at home. Doubtless much might be said on either side, were it in any way desirable to reopen a somewhat bitter controversy. One thing is certain, that nowhere, and at no time, have missionaries of the Church of England, and of the Wesleyan body, found their labours followed by more signal success than in New Zealand; and the zeal, fortitude, and high-souled devotion of the pioneers of the gospel in our Brighter Britain, must surely win the admiration of even the enemies of Christianity.

Not far from Cape Wiwiki, on the northern shore of the Bay of Islands, and half a day's sail away from Kororareka, is a spot of great interest. Sheltered within high craggy headlands, and shut out from the open bay by a rocky and bush-clothed island, is a bright and peaceful little cove. There are but few signs of life here; the place looks almost deserted. A couple of houses are visible, divided by rising ground; and a farm lies round them, bounded by hills wearing the evergreen verdure of the forest.

Walking about this farm, you perceive that it is not of very great extent—a hundred acres or so, probably. But you are at once struck with something that is strange to you, after the pioneer homesteads of the Kaipara. The turf is old and smooth, the fields are drained and level, the ditches are embanked, the hedges full-grown and thick, the imported trees are in maturity. Everything denotes that this is no new clearing. Abundant evidence is all around to testify to the truth of what the hospitable farmer will tell you, namely, that the cultivation here is sixty years old.

This place is Te Puna, ever to be renowned as the site of the first mission, established here by the Rev. Samuel Marsden, in 1814.

The incentives those early missionaries had to go to New Zealand were certainly not of an engaging kind. They knew that the natives were a fierce and bloodthirsty set of savages, that they were constantly at war among themselves, and were addicted to cannibalism. Although some few individuals had visited Sydney, and seemed tractable enough, assuring Mr. Marsden of their good will and power to protect missionaries, yet there was no sort of certainty. The Maoris were known to be badly disposed to strangers, on the whole, and many stories of their treachery were current. Since Marion du Fresne, with fifteen men, was killed by Maoris in the Bay of Islands, there had been various instances of a similar kind. Only a year or two before, the ship *Boyd* had been seized in Whangaroa Harbour, and her company, numbering fifty persons, had been butchered and eaten.

With these facts before their minds to encourage them, Marsden and his brave companions went unhesitatingly into what must have seemed the very jaws of death, resolved to sow the gospel seed in this virgin wild. In December, 1814, the Revs. Marsden, Kendall, King, and Nicholas landed here at Te Puna. Public worship was held here for the first time on Christmas Day.

At that period there was a large population on the shores and islands of the bay, which has since disappeared or moved elsewhere, for the most part. There would seem to have been a considerable kainga either at or near Te Puna. Here, therefore, land was bought, houses and a church of some kind put up, and the mission duly inaugurated. One of the missionaries was actually accompanied by his wife, and she gave birth to a son shortly after they landed. He was the first white man born in New Zealand, and he still resides near the bay, with other families descended from the same parents. Some of us have often partaken of their hospitality.

There is no mission at Te Puna now, and only the two households for population, but the original mission continued there a good many years. Soon after its origination, another station was opened on the Keri-keri river, about twenty miles from Te Puna. Here there is a stone block-house, which was erected for defence, if necessary. It is now used as a store. There is besides a most comfortable homestead, the residence of a family descended from one of the early missionaries. It is a very pleasant spot, with all the air of an English country grange, save and except that block-house, and other mementoes of the past that our hospitable hosts have been pleased to show us.

Some miles along the shore of the bay, from the point where the Keri-keri estuary opens from it, we come to Paihia, at the mouth of the Waitangi. This is directly opposite to Kororareka, from which it is five or six miles distant. Just down the shore is a villa residence, and one or two other houses, indicating the farm of a wealthy settler. A splendidly situated home that, with its glorious view over the picturesque bay, its surrounding gardens and orchards, and its background of woods and mountains. Here was where the first printing-press in New Zealand was set up.

Near by, but opening upon the Waitangi rather than on the bay, is a deep, dark glen. At the bottom of it, and filling the lower ground, are the wharès and cultivations of a good-sized Maori kainga. There are some frame-houses, too, which show how civilized our brown fellow-subjects are becoming. And from here we can row up the winding Waitangi river to another point of interest.

Some miles above, the influx of the tides is stopped by high falls, just as it also is in the Keri-keri river, close to the old station. Waitangi Falls is the port for all the inland country on this side. There is a young settlement here, and the place is remarkable for being the spot where the famous treaty was signed. Moreover, the falls are well worth looking at.

One of the most interesting stories relating to the Bay of Islands is that of the first Maori war, which was waged around it from 1845 to 1847. It has been related often enough, and I can only find room for some very brief details. Such as they are, they are mostly gathered from the oral narrations of eye-witnesses, both English and Maori, whose testimony I feel more inclined to believe than that of some printed accounts I have seen.

Hone Heke was the leader of one of the sections into which the great Ngapuhi tribe had split after the death of the celebrated Hongi Hika, who expired March 5, 1828. Captain Hobson's friend, Tamati Waka, was chief of another section; while Kawiti, another chief, headed a third. These persons were then paramount over pretty nearly the whole region lying between Mongonui and the Kaipara. They had been among the confederate chiefs whom the British Government recognized as independent in 1835; and their signatures were, subsequently to that, attached to the Treaty of Waitangi.

Shortly after the proclamation of New Zealand

as a British possession, Governor Hobson, seeing that Kororareka was unsuited for a metropolis, removed the seat of government to the Waitemata, and there commenced a settlement which is now the city of Auckland. Order had been restored in the former place, but its importance and its trade now fell away.

The Ngapuhi had some grievances to put up with. The trade of the Bay was much lessened; import duties raised the price of commodities; while the growing importance of Auckland gave advantages to the neighbouring tribes, the Ngatitai, Ngapaoa, Waikato, and Ngaterangi, which the Ngapuhi of the Bay of Islands had formerly monopolized. It needed but little to foment the discontent of a somewhat turbulent ruler such as Hone Heke.

In the year 1844 this chief, visiting Kororareka, and probably venting his dissatisfaction at the new regime pretty loudly, was incited by certain of the bad characters, who had previously had it all their own way in the place. They taunted him with having become the slave of a woman, showing him the flag, and explaining that it meant his slavery to Queen Victoria, together with all Maoris. In such a way they proceeded to work up his feelings, probably without other intention than to take a rise out of the Maori's misconception of the matter.

Hone Heke took the thing seriously. He said that he did not consider himself subject to any one. He was an independent chief, merely in alliance with the British, and had signed the Treaty of Waitangi in expectation of receiving certain rewards thereby, which it appeared had been changed into penalties. As for the flag, if that was an emblem of slavery, a Pakeha fetish, or an insult to Maoridom, it was clear that it ought to be removed, and he was the man to do it.

Accordingly, he and his followers then present, marched at once up the hill above Kororareka, and cut down the flagstaff that had been set up there. Then they withdrew quietly enough. The settlers were much disconcerted, having no means of coercing Heke, and not knowing to what this might lead. However, they set the flagstaff up again.

Hone Heke appeared once more with his band, this time in fierce anger. They cut down the restored flagstaff, and either threw it into the sea, or burnt it, or carried it off. Heke also threatened to destroy Kororareka if any attempt was made to fly the British flag again.

H.M.S. *Hazard* now came up from Auckland, where considerable excitement agitated the young settlement. The flagstaff was again restored, and, this time, a small block-house was built round it, which was garrisoned by half a dozen soldiers.

Now, Hongi Hika, previous to his death, had enjoined a certain policy upon his successors. He had told them never to make war upon such Pakeha as came to preach, to farm, or to trade. These were not to be plundered or maltreated in any way. They were friends whose presence could only tend to the advantage of the Maori. But the English sovereign kept certain people whose only business was to fight. They might be known by the red coats they wore, and by having stiff necks with a collar round them. "Kill these wherever you see them," said Hongi; "or they will kill you."

So Hone Heke sent an ultimatum into Kororareka, to the effect that, on a certain specified day, he should burn the town, cut down the flagstaff, and kill the soldiers. The attack was fixed for night, and it came with exact punctuality. Most of the inhabitants took refuge on board the *Hazard* and some other craft then lying in the harbour; while these prepared to guard the beach from a canoe attack. Captain Robertson of the *Hazard*, with some forty marines and blue-jackets, aided also by a party of settlers, took up a position on the landward side of the town.

Hone Heke's own mind seems to have principally been occupied with the flagstaff. The main attack he left to Kawiti, who had joined him, with five hundred men. Heke himself, with a chosen band, crept round unperceived through the bush, and lay in wait near the top of the flagstaff hill, in a little dingle, which is yet pointed out to visitors. Here they lay for some hours, awaiting the signal of Kawiti's attack upon the town below. While in this position, Heke kept his men quiet by reading the Bible to them, expounding the Scriptures as he read; for all these Ngapuhi, whether friends or foes, were professed Christians at that period.

By-and-by, the sound of firing and shouting in the town, together with the blazing of some of the houses, attracted the attention of the soldiers in the little block-house round the flagstaff. Unsuspecting any danger close at hand, they came out on to the hill, the better to descry what was doing below. Then Heke's ambush sprang suddenly up, and rushed between them and the open door of the block-house, thus capturing it, and either killing or putting the startled soldiers to flight instantaneously.

Meanwhile a furious battle was taking place in Kororareka. Captain Robertson and his small force were outflanked and driven in upon the town, fighting bravely and desperately. But the numbers of the Maoris were too great for them to contend with, and Robertson, with half his men, was killed, the rest escaping with difficulty to the ships. Then the victorious assailants rushed upon the devoted settlement, speedily joined by Heke's band on the opposite side. The stores and houses were plundered and set on fire, and soon Kororareka was a charred and smoking heap of ruins, only the two churches being left absolutely untouched. This was the first engagement during the war, and was a decided success for the rebels. The fall of Kororareka took place March 11, 1845; Heke having first cut down the flagstaff in July of the previous year.

The news reached Auckland a day or two later, and something like a panic occurred there. The settlers were armed and enrolled at once, and the place prepared for defence; for it was said that Heke and Kawiti had determined to destroy that settlement as well. Had they been able to march upon it then, it is possible that their attack could not have been successfully withstood, so limited were means of defence at that time.

But Tamati Waka, the stout-hearted friend of the British, led out his section of the Ngapuhi at once, and took up arms against their kinsmen under Heke. He prevented the rebels from leaving their own districts, and thus saved Auckland, allowing time for reinforcements to reach New Zealand, and so for the war to be carried into Heke's own country. All through the campaign he did efficient service on our behalf, contributing much to the final establishment of peace.

Tamati Waka Nene, to give him his full name, had been a savage cannibal warrior in the days of Hongi. On one occasion then he had led a taua, or war-party, of the Ngapuhi far to the south of Hauraki Gulf, destroying and literally "eating-up" a tribe in the Kati-kati district. Subsequently, he embraced Christianity and civilization, but it is evident that the old warrior spirit was strong in him to the last. He was an extremely sagacious and intelligent politician, fully comprehending the advantages that must accrue to his race from British rule. He enjoyed a government pension for some years after the war, and, when he died, a handsome monument was erected over his remains in Kororareka churchyard. It stands not far from where bullet and axe-marks in the old fence still show the spot where Robertson fell.

When Heke found himself pledged to war, he sent intimations to all the settlers living about Waimate, Keri-keri, and the north of the bay, mostly missionary families. He said he had no quarrel with them, and would protect their persons and property if they would trust him. Some remained, and some took refuge in Auckland. Those who stayed were never in any way molested; Heke kept his word to them to the letter. But of those who fled he allowed his men to pillage the farms and houses, by way of utu for not believing him.

As soon as the authorities were in a position to do so, a strong force was sent into the Bay district, to operate in conjunction with Tamati Waka's men in putting down the insurrection. Three engagements were fought, resulting in advantage to the British. The rebels were then besieged in the fortified pa of Ohaeawae, some twenty-five miles inland. No artillery had been brought up, and the consequence was that our troops were repulsed from before this pa again and again, with severe loss. But the victory was too much for the rebels, who suffered considerably themselves, and ran short of ammunition. One night they silently evacuated the place, which was entered next day by the British, and afterwards destroyed. Very similar experiences followed shortly after at the pa of Okaehau.

Finally, in 1847, the insurgents were beleaguered in the pa of Ruapekapeka, situated near the Waitari river. This they considered impregnable, and it was indeed magnificently defended with earthworks and palisades, arranged in such a manner as to excite the wonder and admiration of engineers. A model of it was subsequently made and sent home.

Some artillery had now been got up, with immense labour and difficulty owing to the rugged character of the ground. These guns were brought to bear upon the pa. But the Maoris had hung quantities of loose flax over the palisades, which fell into place again after the passage of a ball, and hid the breach it had made. Thus the besiegers could not tell what they had effected, while the defenders were enabled to repair the gaps unseen.

The pa was taken in rather a curious way. It happened that no engagement had been fought on a Sunday, and the rebels, being earnest Christians, and having—as Maoris have to this day—a respect for the Sabbath, more exaggerated than that of the Scots even, concluded that an armistice was a matter of course. When Sunday morning came, they went out of the pa at the back to hold worship after their manner. Tamati Waka's men, perceiving this, conquered their own Sabbatical leanings, and, finding an opening, rushed into the pa, followed by the British troops. The disconcerted worshippers attempted to retake the pa, but were speedily routed and scattered.

This event terminated the war. The insurgents were broken and disheartened, their numbers reduced, their strongholds captured, and their ammunition exhausted. They soon all laid down arms and sued for pardon. Ever since, all the sections of the rebel tribe have been perfectly peaceable, and take pride in the epithet earned by Tamati Waka's force, "the loyal Ngapuhi," which is now to be applied to the entire tribe.

This first Maori war presents some considerable contrasts to those which had afterwards to be waged with other tribes, in Wellington, Nelson, Taranaki, and Waikato. It was characterized by humanity on both sides, and by an approach to the usages of conflict between civilized peoples. The Ngapuhi had had the missionaries among them longer than any other tribe, and had benefited greatly from their teaching. Some barbarity they still showed, perhaps, but their general conduct was widely different from what it would have been twenty or thirty years before.

At the attack on Kororareka, a woman and several other fugitives were made prisoners. They were treated kindly, and next day Hone Heke sent them on board the ships in the harbour. A settler informed me that he was once conveying wounded soldiers in a bullock-dray, from the front at Ohaeawae down to the bay. On the road, a party of Heke's men suddenly appeared out of the bush and surrounded them. They were quite friendly, however, grounding their arms for a sociable smoke and chat. They counted the wounded soldiers, giving them fruit, and assisting at the passage of a dangerous creek. At parting, they merely reminded the soldiers that if they came back they would be killed, as they, the rebels, intended to kill or drive away all the red-coats.

Waimate is the most important centre to the north of the Bay of Islands; it lies about ten miles inland from Waitangi Falls. The roads from Waitangi to Waimate, to Ohaeawae and Okaehau, are really good. A buggy might even be driven along them with perfect ease. Only, between Waitangi and Waimate there is a formidable creek, the bridge over which is continually being swept away by floods. Then one must cross by a difficult and shifting ford, and, if the creek be full, it may be necessary to swim one's horse over, as once happened to me, I remember.

On proceeding inland in this district, the ground loses its ruggedness. It is not flat, exactly, but it is only gently undulating, and not so violently broken as in most other parts of the north. The soil is volcanic, the ground mostly open, and much of it splendidly fertile, like that of the Bay of Naples. There are extinct craters and old lava streams here and there; but there has been no evidence of activity in them within the memory of man or of Maori tradition. The district of active volcanoes, solfataras, hot-springs, geysers, and so on, lies beyond the limits of the Land of the Kauri altogether.

Waimate was settled by the early missionaries. It includes lands held by the representatives of three parent Societies. It is a large village, composed of residences that may well be termed villas. Nearly all the inhabitants belong to missionary families, and they form a sort of little aristocracy here to themselves. There is a kind of old-world air about the place : it seems to be standing still while the rest of New Zealand is progressing fast and furiously around it. The people are the soul of kindly hospitality, but they are a little exclusive from the very fact of having lived here all their lives, and of having seen but little of the outside world. For the same reason, and because new settlers do not come up, owing to the land not being readily obtainable, they are somewhat averse from movement, and inclined to jog along in a settled groove.

I know of no place in the colony that presents such a striking resemblance to a quiet, stick-in-the-mud, rural locality of the old country. The Europeans are the gentry, and the Maoris round might pose as the rest of the population.

There is a handsome church at Waimate, but

there is no hotel, though there are very good ones at Waitangi and Ohaeawae. There are yards and pens to accommodate a horse, cattle, sheep, and pig-market, which is held here at regular intervals. Waimate is a great farming centre, some of the lands about it having been under the plough for fifty years; still, it is a trifle backward in its modes, the farmers not striving to make a pile, but being content to keep themselves in competence. This may also be esteemed a central point of modern Maori civilization.

There are a number of young families growing up at Waimate, amid the softening influences of its homely refinement. Among them are an unusual number of young ladies. Whatever may be the faults of the place, with regard to its lack of energy and backwardness in farming industry, it redeems them all by the abundant crop of first-class British rosebuds it is raising for the delectation of hungry bachelors.

Well do I remember, once, Dandy Jack rejoining a party of us, who were up at Kawa-kawa on business. There was such a look of beatified content upon his face, that we all exclaimed at it. He told us he had been stopping at a house where there were ten lovely girls, between the ages of fourteen and twenty-six. He had come to bring us an invitation to go and visit there, too. Within half an hour every horse was saddled, and every individual of us, having completed his most killing toilette, was on the road to this bush-nursery of Beauty!

Six or eight miles from Waimate we come to Ohaeawae, a place of very great interest. The most conspicuous object is the beautiful church, whose tall spire mounts from a rising ground in the centre of the settlement. That church occupies the very site of the old pa, and, what is more, it was built entirely at the expense, and partly by the actual labour, of the very Maoris who fought the British here in Heke's war.

With the exception of the principal store and hotel, and possibly of one or two other houses near, Ohaeawae is a Maori town. A few miles further along the road is yet another straggling settlement, whose name I forget, and all is mainly Maori. These natives here are even further ahead than we are in the Kaipara. They have good frame-houses in all styles of carpentering; they have pastures fattening their flocks and herds and droves; they have their ploughs and agricultural machinery; and fields of wheat, potatoes, maize, and what not. They use the telegraph and the post-office for business or pleasure; they have their own schools, police, and handicrafts of various kinds. In short, as a body, they seem quite as much civilized as if they were white instead of brown. I suppose that, round Ohaeawae and Okaehau and Waimate, the Maori may be seen in the highest state of advancement to which he has anywhere attained. But more of him anon.

Between these settlements and the Hokianga waters, the roads become more inchoate again, and one passes through wild land, which gets more and more covered with bush as one proceeds. Hokianga, though it has its history of the early days, in common with the Bay, is far behind it in progress. In fact, Hokianga is a long way less forward than the Kaipara, and there are very few settlers in it. Its principal features are steep and lofty ranges, and a rich luxuriance of forest. The scenery is magnificent.

Winding along down the Waima or Taheke rivers, no eye so dull but must admire the glorious woodland beauties around. Soft green willows sweep the waters, and hide the banks below their foliage like some natural jalousie. Above is a bewildering thicket of beauty. Ferns, fern-trees, fern-creepers, every variety of frond, mingled with hanging masses of white star-flower, pohutukawa trees one blaze of crimson, trees and shrubs of a hundred varieties. And above tower lofty ranges, covered to the topmost summit with dense impenetrable woods, sparkling and gleaming with a thousand tints in the brilliant sunshine and clear atmosphere.

As the boat travels down the stream, teal and wild-duck splash and glide and scuttle and fly before it. The wild birds of the bush, that some will have it are becoming extinct, are here to be seen in greater numbers than anywhere else I know of. Those rare green and scarlet parrots tumble and shriek on the summits of the trees, while the large purple sultana-ducks peep forth occasionally.

Here and there some vista opens, disclosing a little Maori kainga, or the house and clearing of a settler, who thinks more, perhaps, of living amidst such natural beauty than of making a prosaic pile in any less attractive spot. I love the Kaipara, and I am in honour bound to deem Te Puke Tapu on the Arapaoa the acme and perfection of woodland glory—but, in the Hokianga, splendid and magnificent, one forgets other places.

Take that gorge of the main estuary, for example, just above Wirineki, where the Iwi Rua raises its wild peaks, and sends its tremendous shoulders with their ridgy backs and dark ravines, all clothed in overwhelming wealth of forest, rushing down to the blue water. What can one say but that it is simply sublime! As Wales is to Scotland, so is this to the Yosemite.

There is but little industry in Hokianga. There are some sawmills, but they are comparatively small, and do not add very largely to our timber trade. There are some farms, but they, too, are small and doing little. There are schools, but their work is limited.

The principal settlement is Hurd's Point, to which place a steamer comes from the Manukau once a fortnight. It is claimed here that this is actually the oldest settlement in New Zealand, prior even to Kororareka. A man named Hurd came here early in the century, and established a store for trade with the Maoris; sailing vessels from Sydney occasionally communicating with him.

The Point is about sixteen miles from the Heads. There are somewhere about a dozen good houses, two hotels and stores. A gentleman who lives here has even more manifold occupations than our Mayor of Te Pahi. But the population of this, and of the district generally, is mainly Maori, or Maori half-breed. One can trace in Hokianga some reminiscences of the French invasion, of Baron Thierry, and of the Pikopo, as the Maoris term the Roman Catholic mission.

While the civilization of the Maoris has advanced

further here and at Ohaeawae than it has almost anywhere else, it is curious that some very primitive kaingas lie to the north of Hokianga. I suppose that nowhere in the North could you find places where there is less of Pakeha civilization and more of ancient Maori manners, than in one or two of these. They are completely secluded, and have scarcely any intercourse with strangers.

At these places I have been hospitably entertained, in true Maori fashion, and have found a large amount of genial, kindly friendliness. Some of the elders had not forgotten Heke's war, in which they had taken part. It seemed to them to be an event of yesterday only. They spoke of it as of something amusing, a good joke on the whole, and without any apparent feeling that there had been anything serious in it.

Yet these people questioned me eagerly about Akarana (Auckland), and things among the Pakeha. I rose into immense dignity among them because I had seen and could describe Te Kwini (the Queen), Te Pirinti Weri (the Prince of Wales) Te Pirintiti Weri (the Princess of Wales), and Te Pikanini (the young princes and princesses). All the inhabitants of the kainga, men, women, and children, gathered round the fire in front of my wharè to hear what I had to tell them. There was no end to their questions, and a sort of rapturous excitement spread among them as I dilated on the subject of our royal family. I think it would be no difficult thing to raise a Maori legion for foreign service. And I am quite sure that nowhere, in all the realm upon which the sun never sets, has Queen Victoria more devoted and enthusiastic subjects than she has among her "loyal Ngapuhi."

Such is a brief, a very brief account of our most interesting region, crammed as it is with mementoes of the past, that will grow dearer and more valued to this country as time recedes from them. I have but glanced at some prominent features. It would take a volume or two to contain all that might be written.

But when that railway which Old Colonial talks of is completed, I intend to write a guide-book to the three counties, with full historical details. It ought to be a good spec., you know, when crowds of tourists are rushing to "do" our classic ground!

CHAPTER III.

MAORI MANNERS.

I.

OLD COLONIAL says that no book about Northern New Zealand, past or present, would be complete without some special reference to Maori manners. So, with his larger experience to aid me, I am going to try and depict them, in brief and to a limited extent. Perhaps the best way to begin is by sketching the early history of the race, so far as it is known. Also, we will be pedantic for the nonce, and such words of the native tongue as are used shall be free from European corruptions. Thus, to begin with, there being no "s" in the language, which only consists of fourteen letters, and no plural termination, Maori (pr. *mowry*) stands for either one or many, and Pakeha (white man, stranger, pr. *Pah-kay-hah*) signifies either the singular or plural number.*

* See *Pronunciation of Maori Names*, in the Appendix.

The Maori are a Turanian race, belonging to the Polynesian family of the Malay branch. According to their own traditions, they came to New Zealand from some island in the South Sea, known to them as Hawaiiki. Probably they had migrated in the first instance from the Malay Peninsula. A certain number of large canoes landed the pilgrim fathers of the race on the shores of Ahinamaui,* the names of which are remembered, each of the tribes tracing its ancestry to one. The date of this incursion is reckoned to have been about A.D. 1400; the calculation being arrived at by comparison of certain genealogical tally-sticks kept among the tribes.

The Maori would seem to have degenerated from some more civilized condition, as is evidenced by the remains among them of astronomical knowledge, and of a higher political constitution, the basis of which is discoverable in their institution of the tapu. They brought with them to New Zealand the kumera (sweet potato), the taro (bread-root), the hue (gourd), the seeds of the koraka tree, the dog, the pukeko (swamp-hen), and one or two of the parrot tribe. They found in New Zealand an aboriginal race of men, inferior to themselves. They also found several species of gigantic birds, called by them moa, and by naturalists *Dinornis*, *Aptornis*, and *Palapteryx*.

* The North Island.

The Maori, of course, made war upon both man and bird, the latter for food from the first, and the former probably for the same purpose eventually. They had succeeded in exterminating both before Europeans had a chance of making acquaintance with them. Bones of the moa are frequently found, and, till recently, it was believed that living specimens existed in the recesses of forest and mountain. But of the aboriginal race no trace remains, unless, as some have thought, there be an admixture of their blood in the few Maori of Otago and Stewart Island.

New Zealand was discovered by Abel Jan van Tasman, in 1642, to whom it owes its name—a name, by the way, that may one day be changed to Zealandia, perhaps, just as New Holland has become Australia, and Van Diemen's Land, Tasmania. The natives received the Dutch navigator with hostility, massacring a boat's crew. He, therefore, drew off and left, merely coasting for a short distance. No one else visited the country until 1769, when Cook arrived in it for the first time.

Captain Cook was likewise received with hostility by the Maori, on his first landing in Poverty Bay. But afterwards, in the Bay of Plenty, Mercury Bay, and the Bay of Islands, he met with better treatment, and was able to establish friendly relations with certain tribes. He spent altogether nearly a year in New Zealand, between 1769 and 1777, in which last year he left for Hawaii, to meet his death there in Kealakekua Bay. He circumnavigated the islands, which had previously been supposed to form part of a great Antarctic continent. He also bestowed upon the Maori the pig and the potato, and has left us some still interesting accounts of what he observed in the country.

Subsequently to Cook's last visit, and in the intervals between his voyages, other explorers touched here. De Lunéville, De Surville, Crozet, D'Urville, and Du Fresne, the French navigators, followed in the footsteps of Tasman and Cook. Then, too, whalers began to call along the coasts; and, by-and-by, traders from Sydney adventured hither for timber, and flax (*phormium*), and pigs, and smoked heads. But it was a risky thing in those days to do business with the Maori. Any fancied slight or injury was resented most terribly. Several ships were lost altogether, their crews being butchered and eaten; while boats' crews and individual mariners were lost by others.

In 1772, Du Fresne, with fifteen of his men, was killed in the Bay of Islands. He had aroused the wrath of the natives by trespassing on tapu ground; and they also avenged on him an action of De

Lunéville's, who had rashly put a chief in irons. In 1809, the ship *Boyd* was taken in Whangaroa Harbour, and all her company killed, because the captain had flogged a Maori thief. Again, in 1816, we hear of the American brig *Agnes* meeting with a similar fate in Poverty Bay, or thereabouts.

From the end of last century down to 1840, a few individual white men took up their residence among the Maori here and there. These Pakeha-Maori, as they are called, were runaway sailors, or such as had been shipwrecked or made prisoners, or were wild, adventurous characters who preferred the savage life to the restraints of civilization. They married Maori women, raised families, and conformed to all the native customs, sometimes becoming chiefs and leaders in war. When some fitful intercourse was established with Sydney, these men were the medium of trade, and achieved immense importance in that way. It soon became the fashion among the chiefs of tribes for each to have his own special Pakeha-Maori. Force was sometimes resorted to to obtain these men. They were captured and compelled to remain, while wars between rival tribes were conducted for the possession of them. Rutherford, a survivor of the *Agnes*, was one such. His experiences of twelve years' residence among the Maori are recorded in

Lord Brougham's compilation. Judge Maning has related the tale of another, at a somewhat later date.

In 1814, as has been elsewhere mentioned, the Rev. Samuel Marsden, together with some other missionaries, landed in the Bay of Islands; and from that event, New Zealand's real history may be said to commence.

The story of Marsden's interest in New Zealand is not without a certain romantic element. He was chaplain to the Government of New South Wales. At Sydney he had many opportunities of hearing of New Zealand, and of the terrible race of fighting man-eaters who inhabited it. Traders spoke freely of all they knew, and the barbarities, treacheries, and fearful deeds of the Maori, much exaggerated, no doubt, were matters of common report. Moreover, individual Maori sometimes shipped as sailors on board the vessels that touched on their coasts; and so Marsden was able to judge of the character of the race from the actual specimens he saw. We may be sure that he was favourably impressed by their evident superiority in every way to the black aborigines of Australia.

Marsden was in England in 1809, and there he vainly endeavoured to awaken sympathy on behalf of the Maori, and to persuade the Christian public to make effort for their help. On his return, he noticed, among the sailors of his ship, a coloured man, very sick and dejected. Him he made acquaintance with, finding him to be Ruatara, a Maori of the chieftain rank, belonging to the Ngapuhi tribe.

Ruatara had had an eventful time of it. In 1805, when a mere lad of eighteen, he had shipped on board a whaler, hoping thereby to see something of the world. In her he was treated badly, being marooned on a desert island for some months, and eventually brought back again to New Zealand, without more experience than a whaling cruise in the South Sea could give him.

But, nothing daunted by these vicissitudes, he again shipped on board a whaler, and in her was carried to London. This was the acme of his desires, for his great idea was to see King George. But, all the time the ship lay in dock, Ruatara was scarcely allowed to go on shore, even, and was not permitted to carry his wishes into execution. He appears to have been brutally ill-treated, and was finally turned over to a convict ship, the *Ann*, bound for Port Jackson. On board of her Marsden sailed, and saw and took this forlorn wretch, ill and disappointed, under his protection.

Arrived in Sydney, Marsden took Ruatara to his own house, and kept him there as his guest for some months, doing his best, meanwhile, we may be sure, to enlighten the mind of the barbarian whom Providence had thrown in his way. Finally, he took means to send Ruatara home to his own country.

The Church Missionary Society, stirred by Marsden's representations, at last sent out a missionary party. But on their arrival in Sydney the members of it hesitated about venturing to New Zealand—the affair of the *Boyd*, and similar deeds, being just then fresh in the colonial mind. Marsden, however, was not to be daunted.

In 1814 he sent a vessel to the Bay of Islands, loaded with useful presents, and bearing an invitation to Ruatara to visit him once more. It was readily accepted, not only by Ruatara, but also by several other chiefs, including the subsequently famous Hongi Hika, who was uncle to Ruatara. These persons were hospitably entertained by Marsden at his residence at Paramatta. Towards the end of the year, they returned to New Zealand, and with them went Marsden and his companions, landing at Te Puna in December of that year, as has been elsewhere spoken of.

This is the first appearance of the redoubtable Hongi. Both he and Ruatara took the missionaries under their protection, and firmly maintained that attitude as long as they lived. Neither of them embraced Christianity; but Hongi's care for the missionaries is shown in the charge he gave to his successors on his death-bed concerning them, which I have recorded in a previous chapter. Ruatara was a man of much milder disposition than his uncle, though both appeared well-mannered, courteous, amiable, and eminently sagacious when among Europeans. Ruatara would probably have become a convert, had he not died soon after the advent of Marsden.

During this period many of the Maori evinced great desire to travel, and especially to see England and its king. They were ready to undergo any amount of hardship and ill-treatment to accomplish this. Numbers shipped as seamen on board such vessels as would receive them. Sometimes they resorted to amusing tricks in order to get carried to England. Tupei Kupa, for example, a powerful chief in the neighbourhood of Cook Straits, came on board a ship passing along the coast, and resisted all endeavours, even force, to make him return. He was eventually made to serve as a sailor, and seems to have become a general favourite. He resided some time in Liverpool, afterwards being sent home by Government.

Hongi was affected by the same spirit. In 1820 he, accompanied by another chief, Waikato, and under the charge of Rev. Mr. Kendall, visited England. There he was presented to King George, and was made much of. The two chiefs aided Mr. Kendall and Professor Lee in the compilation of the first Maori vocabulary. They returned to Sydney loaded with many and valuable presents.

But in Sydney the true character of Hongi came out. He realized all his property, and converted it into muskets, powder, and ball. With these he sailed joyfully back to his own country. Arrived there, he set about arming his fighting men and instructing them in the use of the new acquisitions. He also became very friendly to such trading vessels as touched on his coasts, giving them cargoes of such produce as the country afforded in return for more arms.

This chief's ambition was to constitute himself king of all New Zealand, just as King George was sovereign over all Britain. His theory of the way to bring this about seems to have been by killing and eating all who opposed the project. There were some thirty tribes of the Maori, and these were divided and subdivided into various little sections. Sometimes a powerful chief was dominant over a large confederation; and, again, each little kainga regarded itself as independent.

Originally, Hongi was ariki (head chief or king)

of the Ngapuhi, and ruled over the inhabitants of the districts round the Bay of Islands, and between that and the west coast. As soon as he had returned from England, and had achieved the possession of fire-arms, he converted his previously somewhat loose lordship into a real despotism. He organized a taua (army, regiment, or war-party), and quickly reduced any unruly sections to obedience. Then he attacked the Ngatipo of Whangaroa, the Ngararawa of Whangape, and the Ngaopuri of the North Cape. These he massacred, devoured, and dispersed, swelling the ranks of his army with accessions from among the subdued tribes.

After this, various expeditions, under the command of Hongi, or his sub-chiefs, marched southward to slay and eat all and sundry. The Ngatewhatua, a populous tribe of the Kaipara districts, had to bear the brunt of Hongi's advance, and were almost annihilated. He penetrated a long way south, ever victorious over every one by reason of his superior weapons. There is little doubt that he must have sometimes led an army of as many as five thousand men, mostly armed with muskets. This was a prodigious force for Maori war, irrespective of the enormous advantage of powder and ball over the native merè (battle-axe) and patu (a sort of halberd).

Such was the spirit of the Maori, and such their warlike ferocity, that tribes never thought of submitting peaceably, or fled from superior strength. They always fought first. It is difficult to realize, nowadays, the awful carnage that Hongi instituted. Districts were depopulated, tribes annihilated, men, women, and children, in scores and hundreds, were butchered and eaten; pa and kainga were burnt and destroyed.

Far to the south went the bloodthirsty conquerors, even into what afterwards came to be the province of Wellington. Ngapaoa, Ngatewaikato, Ngatimaniapoto, Ngatiawa, and many another tribe felt the full force of Hongi's lust for conquest. Even to the East Cape his terrible warriors came, decimating Ngateurewera and Ngatiporu. Of these latter they once roasted and ate fifteen hundred, at a single one of their cannibal orgies.

But Hongi did not become king of New Zealand after all. He received a wound in battle, which brought him to his death in 1828. In spite of his propensities for war and cannibalism, both of which, one may say, were hereditary in the Maori blood at that time, Hongi would seem to have possessed many good qualities. His intellect was quick and vigorous, and would have distinguished him among any people. His ingenuity was great, both in overcoming difficulties and in the arts which the Maori used, or that had been taught him by Europeans. His bravery was undoubted, and was mingled with much large-hearted generosity. He had good impulses, and was singularly affectionate to his own family. To him missionaries and white traders owed the first footing they obtained in the country, and the ability to hold their own there afterwards.

From the period of Marsden's first visit the labours of the missionaries began to bear fruit, and Christianity spread, at first slowly, but afterwards with marvellous rapidity and completeness. Soon after Hongi's death a more peaceful era commenced: arms were less often employed; cannibalism was given up among christianized tribes; and peaceful arts were more attended to. In 1823, a Wesleyan mission was established, first of all in Whangaroa; and, in 1837, a Roman Catholic one was commenced in Hokianga. By 1840 the whole of the tribes of the Maori were professedly Christian, and had relinquished their old warlike customs.

In 1864 there arose a singular religious revival among the Maori, known by the name of Hau-hau. This was just at the period when the Waikato war was concluded, and when certain sections of various tribes in the interior had declared themselves independent under a king of their own election. Hau-hau was instituted by some of the old tohunga (priests, prophets, and medicine-men), mainly from political motives. They said that as there was an English Church, a Scottish Church, and a Roman Church, that there ought also to be a distinctive Maori Church. They accordingly set to work to form one.

Hau-hau consists of a frenzied form of Christianity, mingled with some observances taken from the Mosaic Law, and comprehending old heathenish usages grafted upon the new order of things. From the extraordinary excitement its professors manifest, some people have thought that mesmeric influence had a part in it.

Hau-hau became a political movement, being inseparably connected with the "king" rebellion. The Kingite Maori have given a good deal of trouble in former years, but have now been quiescent for long. Their territory occupies Kawhia county on the West Coast, being bounded by the Waikato, Waipa, and Mokau rivers, and the sea. Their numbers are but few.

Till lately these rebels held themselves wholly aloof from intercourse with the outside world, and threatened any one who should enter their territory. At last they began to bring produce to the nearest

Pakeha market, and to buy stores, though still maintaining their reserve. In 1881 there arose some dispute about land that had been confiscated after the war, but that had not been taken possession of. There was talk of a furious row between the rebels and the settlers. This was magnified by English newspapers into a "threatened Maori war," an absurd piece of ignorance, truly!

The "war" was put an end to the other day, by a few policemen arresting the "King," in the midst of his dominions and surrounded by his subjects, and conveying him off to durance vile at Wellington. A demonstration of Taranaki volunteers was enough. No blood was spilt; no violence offered.

Maori wars are things of the past entirely. When are British journalists going to awake to that fact? Now, settlers outnumber Maori everywhere ten to one. There are roads and railways and steamers, sufficient to convey constabulary to any riotous neighbourhood pretty quickly. But the great point is that the Maori of the present day are decent, quiet, and orderly folk. They are intelligent, and possess as much civilization as would be found in many rural districts of England, Scotland, and Wales—I will not add of Ireland, too, for fear I should be Boycotted! Maori and settler are on perfectly equal terms, and the former know it;

moreover, they are not an homogeneous people, but live scattered in small communities. The Kingites, who are the least civilized, and who profess not to acknowledge our authority, showed what they thought of the possibilities of war by their submission to a party of constables the other day. There is no strength among them to make a war if they wished it, which they are much too sagacious to do. Riots, or brigandage, even, in isolated localities, are less to be feared than similar outbreaks in Lancashire or Staffordshire.

To read, as we did a short while ago, in influential London newspapers, that war with the Maori was again imminent, strikes us as excessively ludicrous. "Our shanty" even regards it as a dire insult, and there was some talk among us of going to war ourselves—with the fourth estate in England. Anyhow, it shows how little our friends at home really know about this land of the blest and the free. Have there not been books enough written about it *yet ?*

There are, it is true, a good many Maori who adhere to primitive custom. Here and there you may find a kainga, containing from a score to a hundred souls, where there is not much apparent advance from the state of things fifty years back. But even here you will find that men and women turn out in European clothes, on occasions of state;

that the children receive schooling of some sort; that there is a surprising degree of intelligence and knowledge of the great world and its ways; and that there is a fervent, and often dogmatic, Christianity among the inhabitants.

On the other hand, there are Maori of a more cultivated condition, and these have no small influence with their less sophisticated compatriots. Maori members sit in both houses of the Legislature; Maori have votes at elections; there are some comparatively wealthy Maori; there are Maori farmers, store-keepers, hotel-keepers, artisans, policemen, postmen, teachers, and clergymen. There are two or three Maori newspapers, partly written by Maori, for Maori to buy and read. They are no longer to be regarded as savages, or as a distinct race, even. They are but one of the classes of our community.

The present total Maori population is no more than 42,819; and the European population is 463,729. In 1874 the Maori numbered 46,016, so they have decreased considerably since then. But it is probable that the numbers six years ago were not taken with the same accuracy as at the last census, so that it would, perhaps, be too hasty to say that the race has decreased by 3000 during the last six years; yet this estimate cannot be very far from the truth.

There is no doubt that the Maori race are dying out, and that with great rapidity. At the beginning of this century—about 1820—the missionaries estimated their numbers to be 100,000, a guess that most likely fell far short of the truth. The frightful slaughtering that followed the introduction of fire-arms had, no doubt, much to do with the diminution of the population, but evidently that can have no effect at the present day; nor have the wars we have fought with certain tribes, subsequent to 1840, been of such a bloody nature as to be set down among the immediate causes of decrease.

It has been too hastily assumed that the Maori were lessening before the advent of Europeans. It has been erroneously supposed that they were half-starved, and that they had no option but to resort to cannibalism. Both conclusions are certainly mistaken ones, I feel convinced.

In the first place, when the Maori came to New Zealand, four or five centuries ago, only a very limited number could have arrived. A long and hazardous voyage must have been undertaken in frail canoes, and it is not to be supposed that an entire nation could have so migrated. Moreover, it is probable that the immigrants were driven here accidentally, by stress of weather, possibly. Otherwise, if they were able to voyage about so successfully in the open ocean, at will, surely they would have kept up communication with "Hawaiiki," or other islands, which we know they did not.

It seems clear, therefore, that but a few people originated the Maori inhabitants of New Zealand, and as these were certainly at one time very numerous, it is apparent that after their coming they had gone on increasing and multiplying. At what period, and for what reason, did this process of increase become checked, and change to one of decrease?

When Europeans first became acquainted with the country, the Maori had by no means occupied the whole of it, or even nearly so, nor had they exhausted its resources for the support of life. They were cannibals; but it has been abundantly proved that they were not so from necessity. Cannibalism was a part of the ceremonial of war and victory—nothing more. It was never looked upon as a mere means of livelihood.

It is true, that the Maori had no animals except dogs and rats, both of which they ate; but flesh is not an absolute necessity of existence. They had fish of many kinds in marvellous profusion; they cultivated assiduously the kumera and taro, alone sufficient for the support of life. Such crops as these hardly ever fail in this climate. Then there was the fern-root everywhere, a regular article of diet with them, and sundry other roots and herbs. Some writers have assumed that when the moa had been hunted down and destroyed, there was no other food available, and so the tribes turned on each other. This is monstrously absurd. There is no evidence to show that moa were ever so plentiful as to have been a principal part of the food-supply. There is plenty of traditional evidence to prove that other and smaller birds were more generally used as diet. There is no proof that the Maori were ever in want of means of subsistence. As matter of fact they were not. They never knew what famine was, in the sense in which it has at times been understood in Western Ireland or the Hebrides.

Now war, at that prehistoric period, was a very different thing from what it afterwards became, when fire-arms were introduced. From the very earliest time, according to their legends, war was the main employment of the Maori. But their wars were not of a kind to cause large devastation. Usually they were Homeric combats, where one or two persons were slain on either side. Vast preparations were made for an event of this kind. Rival tribes mustered all their strength; and, with much ceremony, the taua of each came together at some appointed place. Then for days there was much talking and boasting, and various single duels, resulting in little or nothing. Eventually a general engagement would ensue. Hundreds might take part in it, but rarely were there a dozen or a score of casualties. So we gather from such accounts as have reached us. Incessant though the inter-tribal conflicts were, they were not of such a murderous sort as to cause large general decrease. Extreme old age was a very frequent thing, among even prominent fighting-men, just as now there are numerous very aged Maori.

So, it would seem that neither war nor want were destroying the race before the coming of the Pakeha; consequently it is not surprising to find that the fact of their decreasing at all at that period is no fact, and is but an opinion, a theory, an assumption that appears to be devoid of any foundation whatsoever.

When fire-arms were introduced, general butcheries commenced. Hongi initiated this era. But other tribes eventually obtained the coveted weapon, and then there was a carnival of blood all through the land. Here we find the first real cause for general decrease. These fearful wars must have enormously diminished the numbers of the race.

But when Christianity laid hold of the Maori, and when colonization came after it, there was no longer any reason left for a decrease among the native population, at least, so one would have thought; yet the numbers of the Maori have been growing less and less with startling rapidity. The decrease that is going on now, and that has been going on since 1840, is evidently not owing to war or to want. Other causes for it must be sought for. The first Maori census was taken in 1874, and now another enumeration has been made, showing a considerable falling off since the other. Scarcely an old settler but will tell of districts he knows, where years ago there was a much larger native population than there is to-day. It is evident that, as civilization advances, and as Pakeha grow more numerous in the country, the Maori are disappearing faster and faster.

Many causes have been assigned for this. The anti-alcoholists—of whom we have many eminent and enthusiastic professors in the colony—of course, put drink down as the chief reason. I do not think it is, myself. Some Maori may drink themselves to death, but, so far as my experience goes, I have found them to be remarkably abstemious as a rule. Many Maori will not touch liquor at all; many more will take a little, but decline to drink excessively. As one such remarked to me once—

"Little rum good. Makee jolly, dance, sing!

Much rum bad. Makee sleepy, makee head sore, belly sore, all sore!"

A drunken Maori is comparatively rare in the North, at least, as far as my observation goes. I am rather inclined to take medical evidence on the subject of Maori decrease. Certain diseases, introduced by the Pakeha, have spread among them extensively, and work fatally to their constitutions. The women are thereby rendered less capable of maternity, and the children fewer and more sickly.

A good deal of sentiment has been unnecessarily wasted upon this matter. We do not need to raise a cry of lamentation over the departing Maori. Let him go; we shall get on well enough without him! When the ordinary Englishman refers to the matter, he says—

"They're a splendid race, those *Maries!* and it's a thousand pities they should be dying out so fast!"

With this commonly begins and ends the sum of his knowledge of the matter. Now, the Maori is not altogether such an absolutely superior person. Relatively to some other aboriginal races—the Australian black, for instance, and perhaps most of the North American tribes—the Maori may truly be described as a splendid race; but compared with the Anglo-Saxon, the Maori is nowhere. He cannot match our physical development nor our intellectual capacity, average compared with average.

So, let the Maori go. We do not wish him to, particularly. We are indifferent about the matter. We would not hurry him on any account. Nay, we will even sympathize with him, and sorrow for him — a little. We are content to know that he will make room for a superior race. It is but the process of Nature's sovereign law. The weaker is giving way to the stronger; the superior species is being developed at the expense of the inferior.

In appearance, the Maori strike you favourably. Their features are good, being quite in Caucasian mould, though inclining a little to coarseness. Their heads are well shaped, their bodies and limbs well developed and muscular. They are somewhat long in the back and short in the leg, as compared with Europeans; and both men and women are able to pikau (hump, or carry on the back and shoulders) great weights for long distances.

The colour of the skin varies. In some it is almost a coppery brown, in others a dusky olive. The hair is black or brown, occasionally reddish. The faces are open and intelligent, capable of much expression, and pleasing when in repose. The eyes are large and full, and the teeth naturally of dazzling whiteness and regularity. Some of the young girls are comely and pretty, but as they grow old they often get repulsively ugly.

The average height is perhaps a little over that of Englishmen; but the Maori are seldom over six feet, and not often below five feet six inches. Deformed persons are to be seen in every kainga, where they are looked upon as, to some extent, privileged by their misfortune.

The moku (tattooing) has gone out of fashion, and is seldom seen on young men now, except among very conservative communities. Plenty of the older men, however, show it, and are still proud of it. The women were never marked much, a line or two about the mouth, and on the chin, was all they were allowed.

The moku was not mere ornament or disfigurement. It had a distinct heraldic meaning, and the practice had attained to quite high art. The designs are most elaborate, and were traced with exceeding care. They consist of concentric lines and geometric devices, each pattern having its peculiar signification. The markings are of a blue colour; they are principally displayed on the face and breast; and they are so deeply set that the skin is ridged and furrowed, looking as if carved.

The lower classes had but little moku, the more intricate and elaborate patterns being reserved for men of rank. The higher a chief was, the more elaboration did his moku display. When a man rose in rank, he received additional decoration; just as civilized governments confer orders, crosses, and stars upon distinguished generals or statesmen. Often the face was so covered that even the nostrils, eyelids, and lobes of the ears were adorned with minute tracery.

The operator who was entrusted with the making of the moku, was a man of great importance, though he might be of the lowest rank. The possession of a skilled artist on skin was thought so much of in the old days, that wars were sometimes waged to determine who should benefit by his talent. He was a sort of R.A., and M.R.C.S., and king-at-arms in combination.

This individual had his cases of instruments, little hoe-shaped chisels and gouges and knives, made of sharks' teeth, flint, bone, and wood. Very neat and beautifully finished weapons they were. The pigments consisted of charcoal, a prepared red earth, and the juice of the hinau tree.

The proud and happy patient was laid down on his back, and forcibly held in position by assistants. Then the operator sketched out the pattern on his face with charcoal. Each line or dot was chiselled in with a suitable tool, a wooden hammer being used to send the blade well into the flesh. The blood of course gushed freely forth, and was scraped off with an implement made for the purpose. The pigments were rubbed into the incisions as these were proceeded with. As may well be supposed, the pain was simply excruciating, but it was considered unmanly to flinch from it.

Subsequent inflammation was generally severe, and might last for weeks, while the whole operation would have to be effected bit by bit, over possibly a year or two. To add to the hero's misery, all this while he was tapu, or unclean, and could not touch food with his hands, or live in a wharè (house). Unless he was sedulously attended to by the ladies of his family, as was the proper thing, he would undergo no trifling amount of inconvenience.

The moku served a curious purpose at one time. Clumsy though Maori fingers are, they seem to have a natural aptitude for sketching and carving. So, when the earliest missionaries and others called upon certain chiefs to sign the title-deeds of estates they had bought from them, the Maori did so by drawing little sketches of the moku that adorned their faces. Each said, "That is me, and no one else." These curious autographs are still preserved by the Societies in London.

It was the practice in the old days to preserve

the heads of distinguished men who were slain in battle. This was done by smoking and drying them in such a way as to keep the emblazoned skin intact. As soon as traders began to come from Sydney, they were ready to barter valuable commodities for these relics, which commanded high fancy prices among the museums and curio-hunters of Europe.

Great inducements were, therefore, offered to trading Maori to bring heads into market. The product seemed to be going to bring wealth into the country, and industrial enterprise in this direction speedily quickened. Trading tribes went to war on all sides, in order that the supply of heads might be fully up to the demand for them.

When this resource failed, some ingenious and business-like potentate hit upon a splendid device. Procuring the services of a first-class artist, he caused him to adorn a number of slaves with the most elaborate and high-art designs. Nothing was to be spared; they were to be decorated in the grandest style.

When a ship came that way again, and inquiry was made by her captain as to the ruling prices and possible supply of heads, among other commodities, the new commercial scheme of these simple people was at once propounded to him. The chief caused a row of emblazoned slaves to be marshalled before the trader, and told that gentleman to pick out those he admired. Further, he was assured that such as he deigned to choose should be at once decapitated, their heads cured *secundem artem*, and delivered on board his ship with promptitude and dispatch, at the usual market rates.

The new plan was pronounced kapai (good), and gave universal satisfaction. Not only did it encourage a noble and national art, but the revenue of the kingdom was thereby largely increased. We can hardly realize, perhaps, the intense chagrin of these merry folk when they found that the missionaries discouraged their laudable efforts in this direction, not to mention that those teachers also interdicted the time-honoured custom of anthropophagy. I have often fancied I heard some ancient Maori sighing and lamenting for the good old times, the merry days when he was young!

But, possibly, it is as well that the moku and the head-curing process should be now among the number of lost and vanished arts.

CHAPTER IV.

MAORI MANNERS.

II.

THE Maori tongue is akin to several of the South Sea dialects. The language of the distant Sandwich Islands corresponds most nearly to it. A Maori and a Hawaiian can understand one another to a great extent. It is strange that intervening groups should be inhabited by people of wholly different races, who speak in altogether different tongues.

For ordinary colloquial purposes a sufficiency of Maori is readily acquired, though those who study it deeply discover many difficulties. The alphabet contains only fourteen letters, consequently the sound of many words, expressing wholly distinct ideas, is frequently confusingly similar. The grammar is not overcharged with those bugbears of childhood—moods, tenses, and declensions. The tone and inflection of the voice are used to convey a varied meaning to the same word, in many instances. A sentence will have different significations according to the inflection used in uttering it, and to the gestures that accompany it. The idiom is singular, but rather graceful.

The written language has been constructed by the missionaries and others, as has been done with various other tongues in Polynesia and elsewhere. Bibles and sundry more books have been translated and printed in Maori. In fact, there is beginning to be quite a Maori literature, for, besides translations, there have been published several volumes of Maori legends, proverbs, songs, etc., and there are two or three journals regularly issued in the language.

Most of the rising generation are able to read and write in their own tongue, if not in English also; for they all have been, or go, to school. They cannot readily articulate all our sounds, but education is doing much to remedy this; also, they are rather inclined to adhere to their own idiom, which is, of course, to be expected. Very few of the elder Maori have these Pakeha accomplishments, or care to exercise them. A queer pride and prejudice keep them from attempting to learn or speak English. But I have found that a good many of them know a great deal more than they are disposed to allow.

The ancient Maori would seem to have had

some notion of hieroglyphic or picture-writing. The moku is one example of this, and others are to be found in the symbolic carvings of door-lintels and of standard posts, inscriptions on rocks and trees, and the sacred whalebone staves of the tohunga, whereon were kept a genealogical record of the families of high rank.

Oral tradition was well kept up among the Maori, and certain of them may be termed deep scholars in it. They are a long-winded race, and very great at a korero (talk or debate), without which nothing was or can be done. They can reel off immeasurable quantities of legendary history or romance, in prose and verse, having astounding memories for this sort of thing. Oratory was cultivated as an art by them, and many are remarkably eloquent; but the style of their orations principally consists in the recitation of proverbs and traditions, and the application of them to affairs of the moment. Sir George Grey is, perhaps, more intimately acquainted with these things, and with the Maori language, than any other Pakeha, and he has collected and published some of their poems and sayings.

Decidedly the most noteworthy Maori institution was that of the tapu. It exists in various forms throughout the South Sea. There is the tambu of

Fiji, and the tabu of other islands, essentially the same thing. But it was among the Maori that it appears to have been brought to its greatest perfection. We have drawn from it our word *taboo*, which we use to express anything that is rigidly forbidden or disallowed. But the Maori tapu went far deeper than that. To use the words of another writer, "it comprised everything that we would call law, custom, etiquette, prejudice, and superstition, and had therefore its good as well as its bad effects."

Except in some of its superstitious aspects, the tapu is now a thing of the past, and is spoken of here as such. I have not studied the subject very deeply, but have picked up enough knowledge of it to enable me to give a general idea of what it was.

Tapu appeared under many different phases, and was intimately connected with all the concerns of life. A river was tapu at certain well-known seasons, thus providing a close time for the fish. No person might disturb it in any way; no one might fish or bathe in it; nor might a canoe venture upon its surface until the tapu was removed.

A wood was tapu, in like manner, when birds were nesting, tawhera fruit maturing, or rats multiplying. This was in effect a game-law. Similarly, the fields and gardens, the cultivations of kumera and taro, used not to be fenced until the introduction of pigs rendered that necessary. Human trespassers were kept off by means of the inviolable tapu. Burglars and thieves were prevented from entering empty houses, or from appropriating property, by the same simple means.

The application of the tapu was exceedingly simple. A carved and painted rod was stuck up; a bunch of flax was prominently displayed; a rag from the person, a bone, a bunch of hair set in some conspicuous situation, any of these were sufficient indications of the awful mystery. But to remove the tapu was a wholly different matter. That could not be done so easily. In all cases of importance a whole ritual had to be gone through before the tapu could be lifted. Ceremonies of high import were sometimes necessary, even a sort of propitiatory sacrifice seems occasionally to have been made. The karakia, a kind of invocation or prayer, had to be uttered with due solemnity, and this necessitated the intervention of the tohunga.

Here let me explain who this personage was. Like poets, the tohunga was born, not made. What gave him his particular sanctity or dignity, how he was chosen, set apart, or elected to office, are things that no Pakeha can understand. They are sublime and fearful mysteries, into which not even the greatest friend of the Maori has ever been able to penetrate. All we have ever learnt regarding the tohunga is simply that there he *was*, the acknowledged priest, prophet, seer, sorcerer, medical man, judge and jury, executioner, and general adviser of the tribe, while also being the grand vizier of the chief, if indeed he was not the chief himself. He might belong to any class. He might be an ariki (sovereign), a tana (noble), a rangatira (gentleman), or one of the commonalty. He might even be a kuki (slave), or, as has been known, a wahine (woman). This, then, was the individual with whom rested the imposition or lifting of the tapu, in all the more solemn cases, and he was the arbiter and arranger of all its various and intricate modes of application.

The penalties for infringement of tapu depended upon the particular phase of it that was broken. Often instant death was dealt out to offenders; it was inevitable in all important cases. But slighter punishment was sufficient in instances of a less comprehensive kind. Tapu was rarely broken except through accident or ignorance, for dark and gloomy horrors of a spectral kind hovered round it in Maori imagination. Yet if tapu was infringed, neither ignorance of it, nor unavoidable accident was held to be the slightest excuse. Bloody massacres have taken place, and furious wars been waged, simply to avenge some unintentional breach of tapu.

No notion of chastity seems to have belonged to Maori women. They were children of nature, and by no means prudish. Whilst young and free, unengaged to any gentleman, a Maori girl was permitted to have as many followers as she liked, and she was not exactly what we should term virtuous. If pretty she was a general pet in the kainga, and a merry time she had of it. One of the ordinary rules of hospitality as practised in a Maori village, still not entirely obsolete in some places, proves the engaging openness of manners and unrestricted freedom which prevailed socially. The number of half-breed children occasionally seen about a kainga, show the easy way in which certain Pakeha have fallen in with Maori customs.

But tapu provided a marriage law of singular stringency. So soon as a girl was married, nay, merely betrothed, no more license for her. She was tapu to her husband, and if the terrors of the unseen world should not be enough to keep her in the straight path, death was the penalty for the slightest deviation therefrom. She was the slave as well as the wife of her lord, and this continued until, and sometimes even after, his death, unless he should permit a sort of formal divorce.

The person of an ariki was highly tapu. The sublime essence rested, if anywhere, most particularly in his head. His hair might not be cut or dressed without the observance of most formal etiquette. It was a fearful breach of tapu to pass anything over or above his head. Any man was tapu, or unclean, if he were wounded, sick, or undergoing the moku. He might not enter a house, or eat food with his hands. But an ariki in this condition was, of course, tapu in much higher degree. One such dignitary, entering the canoe of another person, accidentally scratched his toe with a splinter. Blood flowing from the wound made the boat tapu, and it thereby became the property of the chief. The owner surrendered at once, not even dreaming of complaint.

Burial places were naturally tapu. A Maori of the olden time would rather die than break their sanctity; and his descendants of the present day have hardly got over the feeling. They were called wahi tapu, and no one dared to enter them. The tohunga and his assistants passed within them to bury the dead, but only with much karakia and ceremony. Spirits of some kind were supposed to keep watch and ward over them, and to wreak terrible vengeance upon trespassers. Water flowing from a wahi tapu was sacred, and whatever it touched became tinctured with the same dread property. Rather a nuisance, sometimes, one would think, such as when a storm of rain should send a new watercourse from some wahi tapu on a hill-side down into the river, or through the kainga. Either would thus be rendered tapu, and have to be deserted at once.

Certain lands, at the present day, cannot be bought from their Maori owners because of wahi tapu upon them. It will be remembered that our show-place is in this category. There is a wahi tapu, a cavern in this instance, near the Bay of Islands, that will yield treasure-trove to curio-hunters some day. With the bodies of the dead were placed their arms, valuables, and personals generally. There is said to be a great store of such riches in this place. Of course, no Maori will go very near it, and the few Pakeha of the district who know its whereabouts would not break the tapu, having too much to lose, and not caring to risk Maori wrath.

In the earliest days of intercourse with Europeans, the tapu was sometimes made useful in business; useful, that is, to the Maori, but certainly not to the trader. For instance, a Sydney vessel sails into Hokianga, or some other river, and is boarded by the ariki of the neighbourhood. This gentleman is perfectly satisfied with the trader's goods, but cannot agree as to the price to be paid for them in pigs, lumber, and flax. The Pakeha wants so much; the Maori offers so little. Long chaffering results in no better understanding. At length the chief departs indignantly, previously putting the tapu upon the ship and her cargo. No other natives will now approach or do business; even other tribes will not infringe the tapu. If the skipper wished to sail off to some other part, he could not do so, except by risking a battle, or spoiling his chances of future trade. Generally, he would come to terms with the chief, after an exasperating delay.

The mana (power) of an ariki was very great; and, in a lesser degree the next ranks, the tana and rangatira, possessed it also. As there was little or nothing externally to distinguish the greatest of chiefs from the meanest of his subjects, " the dignity that doth hedge a king " was conferred and kept up by the mysterious agencies of the tapu. Possibly this was a good reason for its universal supremacy.

The tapu descended into the commonest details of daily life, and it reached to the most solemn and obscurest depths of the Maori mythology. It was a law—a code of laws, based on superstition, elaborated with diplomatic skill, enforced by human justice, universally and entirely accepted, and in its most important aspects was invested with the grimmest terrors of the unseen world.

A Maori would certainly rather die than enter the precincts of a wahi tapu; his terrors would probably kill him if he were so much as touched by a ngarara, or little green lizard. Incredible as it may seem, the Maori were indeed sometimes killed by fear. Instances are on record of individuals who have unknowingly violated the tapu, in some one of its important phases. No one else might be aware of the crime, so that the culprit would have nothing to dread from human justice. But he has been so absolutely terror-stricken, that he has gone straight away into the bush, laid down, and died there.

Everything about an ariki was invested with a sacred mystery. His clothes, weapons, ornaments, or house could not even be touched by the inferior. He must eat alone, could not carry food, could not blow the fire, could not do many things, lest his tapu should unwittingly slay some unfortunate person, or his mana become impaired.

The law of the tapu made government possible among the Maori, and bound them together in their tribes; just as the law of Moses made government possible among the Hebrews. Indeed, in many of its applications the tapu is strangely similar to the Jewish code. Sometimes it may seem ridiculous to us in certain of its forms, so do many of our customs seem ridiculous to the Maori. The other day, one of the Maori members of the House of Representatives rose in his place to oppose a motion for an hour's adjournment of business. He said that the Pakeha system of adjourning for refreshment every now and then was a ridiculous one. Honourable members went and got more or less drunk—so the Maori alleged—and then returned only to wrangle or go to sleep. It would be better to conclude the business on hand, and do the drinking afterwards, observed this sapient legislator. Some "teetotallers'" organ, commenting on the incident, said "his remarks actually shamed the House into decent behaviour for a day or two."

The early missionaries made a dead set against the tapu as a heathen custom, and herein, I think, their policy was a mistaken one. But its whole working was not known to them at that period, and, besides that, it caused them no inconsiderable annoyance. The following story is recorded—by a writer who was himself one of the missionaries—of the first serious blow that heathenism received in New Zealand, and from which originated the acceptance of Christianity by all the tribes of the Maori.

An early party of missionaries had settled at Keri-keri, in the Bay of Islands district, and were on friendly terms with the natives. But when the customary tapu of the Keri-keri river was in force, it caused the mission people great annoyance. The river was their only road, and they could not now pass up or down it; their communications with Te Puna, the principal mission centre in the bay itself, were thus stopped. Stores were required, and at last, in defiance of the native tradition, the mission boat was manned and rowed down the river, thus breaking through the inviolable tapu.

The rage and terror of the Maori were excessive, as may be supposed, and they looked to see the outraged atua (spirits) exterminate the rash Pakeha. But nothing happened, so the Maori determined to avenge the insult themselves, as their fathers had done on Du Fresne, for a very similar violation of tapu. They seized the mission boat on its return, and tied up its occupants preparatory to killing and eating them. Then a whole tribe divided the boat's cargo among themselves.

Now, it so chanced that the bulk of the stores, which the boat was bringing up from Te Puna to Keri-keri, consisted of two items: pots and tins of preserves of different kinds, and a supply of medicines. The Maori devoured the first greedily, and then, as they did not know what else the drugs could be intended for, out of a mere sense of consistency they swallowed salts, jalap, ipecacuanha, castor oil, and so on, as greedily and copiously as they had the jams and pickles.

The result may readily be imagined. Dire prostration of that unhappy tribe. Instant release of the captives, amid the grovellings and supplications of the now anguished and disordered Maori. Triumphant and unexpected victory of the missionary mana. That tribe became instant converts, and were received into the fold of the Church. Had not the missionaries broken through the dreaded tapu unharmed? And had not the avengers of their insulted deities been visited with strange and awful punishment for their presumption in daring to meddle with these Pakeha? What further evidence was needed to demonstrate the superiority of the missionaries over all the Maori gods and devils?

Most strange, too, is another circumstance that operated to the same end. The Maori had oracles, or some kind of divination that was practised by the tohunga. Again and again were these oracles consulted, as to whether the Pakeha religion or the Maori mythology was best worthy of belief. The answer was invariable—so the missionaries tell us. It declared Jesus Christ to be the only true God. So the tapu Maori was set aside; and, little by little, the tapu Pakeha, or Christianity, replaced it.

At the present day all Maori are professed Christians, and, as a rule, very earnest ones. Among the younger there is a state of mind more approaching to our standards, but with the elders it is different. They were born under a different *régime*. Their young minds were filled with hereditary impressions that conversion has been naturally powerless to shake off altogether. Their vague and foggy mythology is still believed in, though they formulate their notion of it in Scriptural words and phrases.

They have long laid aside the old habits of war and cannibalism, but political necessity brought this about, quite as much as Christianity. And the old warlike spirit is by no means dead, any more than the dark and gloomy mysteries of the ancient belief. These crop out sometimes from beneath the veneer of the newer mental garment.

It was believed that the spirits of the dead—of the good dead, the brave warrior dead, apparently—had a long and toilsome journey before them. They had to cross mountains and marshes, and to find their way through forests and over rivers. Many terrible difficulties had to be encountered, and all sorts of spirit foes were ready to contest the narrow path. At last the end of the earth was reached, Cape Reinga, in the extreme north. An awfully tapu place this to living Maori. Here came the spirits of the dead at last, after accomplishing their journey, beset as it had been with many perils. And from the top of Cape Reinga, a mighty rock projecting into the sea, they took their last look at earth and dived into the water. Then they had to swim out beyond the Three Kings Islands, where the gate of Paradise was supposed to be situated.

Many a tattooed Christian cannot give up his belief in this idea, and he still retains it, reconciling it in some dim way with his new theology.

There is a little emerald-green lizard in the bush, called by the Maori ngarara. It is dreadfully tapu, and an old warrior would rather die than touch it. It is believed to contain a spirit, some say an evil demon, others the ghost of a wicked man. There is some uncertainty on that point, even among the most learned tohunga. At any rate it is most excessively tapu. It seems that to throw a ngarara at a Maori, or even to bring it near him, or show it to him, is a crime of a very heinous character. Wars were the consequence of such acts, once upon a time. I did not know of this superstition regarding the ngarara, and nearly lost my life in consequence. At least, I have been told the case was as bad as that.

This was the way of it. Once, when engaged in land-surveying, I had a gang of Maori workmen, to cut the lines through the bush and do the general work of the party. Among these were two or three half-breeds, youngish men, and a couple of old moku Maori, with others. The two old fellows always struck me as being more like Irishmen of the peasant class than anything else. They always had some whimsical joke or another, there was a normally comic look in their faces, and they possessed that quaint affectation of childishness, and love of laughter, which are proverbially characteristic of the Irish peasant.

We had been some weeks out, and had got on very well together. Like all the others, the two old boys were remarkably pious. They had a sort of Bible-class and prayer-meeting every night and morning in the camp. I used to call them "the two apostles," because their baptismal names happened to be Pita (Peter) and Pora (Paul).

One day, when we were all at work on the line, I happened to pick up a pretty little ngarara. Without thinking of what I was doing, I held it out to Pita and Pora, who were nearest to me, asking them what it was, and finally I threw it lightly towards them, saying, "Catch!"

The two apostles became suddenly transformed. They yelled, they screeched, they leapt and danced, they chanted the terrific war-song of their tribe. Never shall I forget the sudden and fierce convulsion that completely changed every feature of their faces and bodies. I no longer knew my two apostles, they had changed into demoniac savages in a whirlwind of wrath.

I stood admiringly watching them, never supposing this exhibition was real, but imagining it was simply a new joke got up for my behoof. The two came gradually closer towards me, clashing their axes together, and seeming like a pair of ferocious panthers. But I noticed that the rest of the gang had stopped work and were looking on. They were not laughing, but seemed excited and concerned. Then it occurred to me that something was not right, and that it would be as well to withdraw.

Just as Pita and Pora were brandishing their axes within a few feet of me, yelling and dancing, or rather bounding, towards me, the two half-breeds rushed swiftly past them and threw themselves between us. Without a word they seized me by the arms and dragged me into the thicket. Then they explained, saying—

" Run for your life! They mean to kill you! "

When I rejoined the working-party an hour or two later, Pita and Pora were calm again, and had resumed their work. They merely growled and menaced me. Afterwards, when we were lying side by side in camp, Pita reverted to the matter as a pleasant episode. He told me all about the ngarara, how tapu it was, and what a dreadful insult I had unwittingly put upon him and his mate. He said they would certainly have killed me in their wild gust of passion, though they would have been sorry for it afterwards. It was all over now, he added, because he and Pora had had time to reflect, and remembered that I was a poor ignorant Pakeha who knew no better. Besides, they were Christians, which they had forgotten in their heat. Now, they were my two apostles once more. I understand that Pora alluded feelingly to the matter during an exposition of the Scriptures, with which he favoured the rest of the gang the following Sunday.

At the present day, the rites and ceremonies of the tohunga have entirely given place to Christian observances; and, as is the wont of primitive intelligences, the Maori are most rigorous observers of all outward forms, whatever degree of fervour they may have spiritually attained. In the young days of Christianity here, the converts ascribed to the missionaries a magical mana, such as they had formerly believed to reside in the tohunga. This was the natural result of that terrible day of wrath on the Keri-keri, when a "great awakening" was brought about through the instrumentality and efficacy of Epsom salts, and when the mana of the tapu Pakeha was thereby so fully demonstrated. Consequently, the ceremonial prescribed and the doctrines inculcated by the missionaries were most unquestioningly accepted.

The Maori adopted religion with a marvellous zeal, and, had it not been for European colonization, sectarianism, and other reasons, they might have become a startling example of fervid Christianity. The differences between denominations, even in the early days, created much bitterness, and, as we have seen, led to Hau-hau. It has needed, at times, all the mana of the missionary, and more, to prevent actual hostilities between communities professing the differing creeds of the Episcopal, Wesleyan, or Roman Catholic bodies. One often meets with sad examples of sectarian animosity manifested among these simple people.

In the early days the missionaries were a political power. Long before the Treaty of Waitangi was signed they had attained a supreme and widespread influence among the tribes. As has been already noticed, it was their desire to have formed a Christian Maori nation, under their own ægis; and, to effect this, they seem to have disregarded the wants of their own countrymen. But all this is retrospective matter, with which it is not now necessary to deal. Neither may I revert to the action of missionaries in the young days of the colony, either with regard to the general government, or to the land-sharking attributed to certain of their number. Too much acrimony has been given rise to already by the discussion of such topics.

The missionary influence has now less practical power, perhaps, than clerical direction in England. Only among secluded hapu (communities) is anything resembling the old force to be found, and there it is necessarily limited and localized. It is felt more among the elders than among the younger generations, who have learnt to read and write, have mixed more with Pakeha, and whose minds are consequently more open, and less inclined to accept spiritual authority as absolute. Their conceptions are not the same as their fathers', to whose minds Christianity came as a new form of tapu, and to whom the missionary appeared as possessor of a more powerful mana than the tohunga.

Sunday is a kind of tapu day with the Maori. They are often more Sabbatarian than Scotsmen, and more pharisaic than the Pharisees themselves. To the letter of the law they pay the minutest attention, whether they estimate its spirit rightly or not.

But there is great diversity of character in this as in other matters, and what is recorded of one tribe or community will not always apply to all. The perfect equality with the Pakeha that the Maori enjoy, and the degree of education that has grown up among them, have produced effects. Among others is a gradual change from fervour to hypocrisy, and from an exaggerated piety to a lesser regard for the forms of religion. Year by year fewer tales will be told of Maori affectations, simple pieties, or childish formalism.

Religion is often the fashion in some of their communities, and is entertained with the most rigid observance. Travellers coming to a Maori kainga upon a Sunday, have been denied shelter and food until sunrise on Monday; and, when Monday came, they have been cheated by the same tattooed Pharisees, who were too sanctimonious to sell a potato to a hungry traveller upon the Sabbath, or to help him build a hut as shelter from the wind and rain.

Maori look upon a money collection in church as a part of the ceremony, on no account to be omitted. The service, they think, is incomplete without it. But they will not give more than one penny, on any account whatever. The warden, who is taking round the plate, has to make change for numerous sixpences, shillings, and even notes (£1) in the course of his progress through the church, in order that the Maori may give their pennies—no more and no less. If a man or woman cannot raise a penny, he or she will usually stop away from church altogether, rather than be remiss in the important ceremony of putting a copper in the plate. In the rare case, when one is found in church without possessing a copper to give, he will *make believe* to put something in the plate when it comes to him, and—by way, I suppose, of strengthening the deception—will make a horrible grimace at the collector.

There are many very quaint scenes to be witnessed in connection with a Maori church, which, until they were used to them, must have sorely tried the gravity of the missionaries and the white part of the congregation. The Maori behave with an exaggerated decorum and seriousness of deportment that is in itself sufficiently laughter-provoking, especially since their eyes are always roving stealthily round to see who is observing them. They sing with such earnestness that at times it almost amounts to fury; and they join in the responses with loud and emphatic fervour. They will weep abundantly and noisily when moved thereto by certain prayers, or by pathetic incidents from Scripture history; or they will laugh uproariously at passages that tickle their fancy.

Nothing whatever can keep these simple and

excitable people from showing their feelings, as aroused by Scripture reading or by the sermon. They listen to the preacher precisely as they do to their own traditions, when told by a native storyteller in the wharè. Their ejaculations are frequent, and prove the intense and vivid interest they take in the stories told them. I have seen a church-ful of Maori grinding their teeth, stamping their feet, waving their arms, and actually raging, when the treachery of Judas was being related to them.

On the other hand, I have seen the same people violently nodding their heads, grinning with appreciation, exclaiming kapai! (good), and showing thorough approbation, over the somewhat questionable business transactions of the patriarch Jacob with Esau and Laban. The stories of Daniel and the lions, and of the other young men who were thrown into the fiery furnace, are high favourites with the Maori. The lions' den finds a parallel in their own mythology, and is recognized by them as being meant for the mysterious cave of the Taniwha, or gigantic lizard-dragon, of which they possess legends.

Dress is a most important item of Sunday ceremony among the Maori, and it is astonishing how well they will turn out. In the seclusion of their own kainga they frequently lay aside civilized attire, and are seen either quite naked, or only loosely enveloped in a dirty blanket; but elsewhere they usually wear shirt and trousers, much the same as settlers. To go to church, as also on high-days and holidays, they appear in wonderfully correct costume; for most Maori have earned money enough, at one time or another, with which to rig themselves out at the stores. Coats of broadcloth, alpaca, or light silk; snowy shirt-collars and cuffs; dangling watch-chains, with perhaps a bouquet in the button-hole, and a bright-coloured satin scarf; "billy-cock" or "wide-awake" hats, white cork helmets, or possibly even a "chimney-pot" hat; accurate trousers and unquestionable boots; in such guise does the Maori rangatira of the present day saunter into church, side by side with the far less well-got-up English-born New Zealand gentleman.

Only one item of the old barbaric splendour—besides the moku on the face—is retained, and that is nearly always seen; namely, the earrings and ornaments. These are prominent features, and their size causes them to be well displayed. The ear ornaments are of considerable variety. A polished slip of greenstone (jade), about six or eight inches in length, is most highly thought of. Then there are dog's teeth, boar's tusks, polished shells and pebbles, bunches of soft white feathers like marabouts, fresh flowers, and yards upon yards of streaming ribbon. But this ornamentation is not unsightly, though at first it may seem somewhat incongruous with the rest of the costume. Some of us used to discuss the advisability of decorating our own ears in the same way, with a view, perhaps, of looking more attractive in the eyes of the Maori maidens.

The Maori young ladies are not, perhaps, strikingly beautiful—our Rakope always excepted—but they have good features, plump, graceful figures, and an altogether comely and agreeable *tout ensemble*. Their white teeth and juicy lips, sparkling eyes and dimpling cheeks, ever-ready smiles and roguish glances, make them a very pleasant sight to see. One loses all distaste for the brown complexion, and even for the two or three lines of moku on the chin, though most of the present generation are without those marks.

The dress of a Maori girl, under ordinary circumstances, is a print frock and nothing else, unless it be a straw hat. But, like the gentlemen, she can come out a grand swell sometimes. You may see all the latest Auckland fashions in a Maori church. The general run of the girls' costume is a dress of calico or some similar stuff, clean and well put together, with a tartan shawl of the most vivid hues over the shoulders, a jaunty hat decorated with flowers and feathers, and a general profusion of natural flowers and fluttering ribbons in the flowing hair. Boots and socks are worn on such occasions, much to the wearers' discomfort, I believe.

But the rangatira girls have learnt from the Pakeha ladies to indulge a passion for fine clothes, and it is seldom that they do not find means to gratify their vanity. A Maori *young lady*—for the rangatira hold themselves as of gentle blood at the very least —has several ways open to her of acquiring sufficient pin-money to place her wardrobe on a proper footing. The first and easiest method is evidently to worry "papa" into selling some of his land; but the Maori paterfamilias is not always pleased to allow his daughters to interfere with his own peculiar line of business.

Of course miss declines to go out to service as a domestic in any settler's family, even if she were fitted for such a post—that is menial work, and suitable only for the inferior kuki girls. But she does not always object to do open-air labour about a farm, dig potatoes and kumera, reap and shell maize, assist among the flocks at shearing time, and take a job of humping. Often she will go gum-digging or flax-picking—one or other of these is her favourite means of raising the wind, unless she can find a market for fish, fruit, or eggs. Any way, get money she must, and will, and does, somehow or another, and on Sundays and gala-days she will appear at church or at the settlement arrayed in a style that would do credit to Regent Street.

At our bush-balls the Maori girls appear in muslins, ribbons, silks, and laces—though these may not always be of the cleanest or newest. And I have even seen silk stockings—white or pink, with "clocks" up the sides—and sandal-shoes upon their feet.

Nor is our modern Maori belle merely a dressed-up savage. Educated at the mission or government schools, she can always read and write in Maori, and often in English better than she can speak it. She has some idea of elementary arithmetic, geography, and history, and can use a needle and thread, study the English fashion-books, and sometimes even use her pencil and draw a little. Still, I am bound to say, all these improvements are but superficial; the Maori blood is in the girl and is bound to show itself, however far advanced may be her education.

Whilst young and unmarried, and even in the early days of matrimony, the Maori girl's life is happy enough. She is petted and caressed by everybody, particularly if more than ordinarily comely; but in the after years she becomes a beast of burden, a hewer of wood and drawer of water, an inferior being, who may be soundly thrashed when her lord considers it good to do so. And the less said about the older women the better; they rapidly pass through every degree of homeliness, until they at last attain to a surpassing and appalling hideousness. In the best and foremost of the Maori girls of the period there is a constant struggle between the acquired Pakeha refinements and the primitive habits of the kainga. This leads to many ludicrous scenes, two instances of which I will describe.

One Sunday I saw the young and handsome daughter of a chief of some rank stepping out of church, and got up to death in a costume that was evidently the result of a recent visit to Auckland itself. For the benefit of my lady readers I will try to describe her dress—so far as an ex-bushman may essay such a task.

Her robe was of pale green silk, adorned with lace trimmings, darker green fringes, and pale pink satin borderings. It had a panier and train, and was shaped and fitted with great taste, and as a fashionable milliner might turn it out. The lady wore cuffs and collar of white lace, with pink satin bows, also a gorgeous cameo brooch, a gold watch-chain, and lavender kid gloves. Her head was adorned with a wide-brimmed white hat, high-crowned, and having one side looped up. It was ornamented with dark green velvet, some gay artificial flowers, a stuffed humming-bird, and a long drooping ostrich feather. Her hair was elaborately dressed in the latest type of chignon; in one hand she carried a gorgeous parasol, all ribbons and fringes and lace, and in the other she had a large feathery fan; while from beneath the white edge of her petticoat two pretty little boots peeped out.

Of course my lady was the cynosure of all eyes, and her delighted vanity was boundless. She minced and rustled down the pathway like a peacock, utterly disdaining all her kindred, male and female, and immensely proud of her own "Englishness." She tossed her head and twisted herself about as a child would do, and wore on her face a chronic smile of supreme self-contentment, while her eyes were wandering all about to note the effect her grandeur was producing.

As her ladyship would not condescend to let any one speak to her, so grand and dignified did she feel, it happened that, when she got to the outskirts of the settlement, she found herself alone, and then, I suppose, her assumption of Englishness suddenly left her. One or two of us had stolen after her, keeping hidden among the bushes at the side of the road, and thence witnessing what followed.

Presently appeared on the scene two or three old Maori women, horrible, repulsive-looking hags, scantily draped in the filthiest and most ragged of blankets, their brows thatched with disgusting masses of hair and dirt. These witches gathered round the young belle, loudly expressing their admiration, and fingering over her Pakeha attire. Then her ladyship experienced a sudden revulsion of feeling, and returned all at once to the level of common humanity. Relinquishing all her airs and graces, she whipped up her silken skirts, squatted down on her hams, drew out a short black pipe, and, cheek-by-jowl with her ancient compatriots, enjoyed a hearty smoke, while relating with great animation the events of the morning.

On another occasion I was riding down to the Bay of Islands, when I came up behind a couple who were riding leisurely along in the same direction. Save and except their shaggy, ungroomed horses, they might have just ridden out of Hyde Park into the middle of that wild country. One was a lady, attired in an elegant, blue, velveteen riding-habit, with hat and feather to match, and with silky brown hair falling over her shoulders down to her horse's croup. Her cavalier, from the top of his white helmet down to his spurred boot-heels, was got up with considerably more regard to effect than is ordinarily seen in the bush.

And there was a good deal of spooning going on, apparently, though that is not so uncommon when couples ride out together, even in the bush. The gentleman was carrying the lady's parasol and other paraphernalia, was leaning over, holding her hand, looking into her eyes, and all the rest of it.

" Ho, ho! " I thought to myself, " that will be Miss Dash, I presume, whom the Blanks expected to visit them. And who is the fellow, I wonder ! "

So I rode quickly after them, coming up without attracting attention, my horse's unshod hoofs making scarcely any noise on the soft road. To my amazement, the amorous pair turned out to be Henere Tangiao, a half-breed, who had been the foreman of a gang of native labourers I had lately discharged; and his fair companion was his very recent bride, formerly Miss Mata Akepiro.

They greeted me with great cordiality, only a little overcome by self-consciousness of their " store-clothes," that had been donned to do honour to some settlers they had been to visit. Said Mrs. Tangiao to me, showing her pretty teeth, and with only a little more Maori accent than I am able to reproduce—

"You come see our house, Mitta Hay; you come see old Maori kainga at Matapa? You come plenty plenty soon, good!"

I accepted the invitation, and did go some days after that. The house was a little wooden cottage, built outside the enclosed kainga of raupo wharè, or reed-grass cabins, of the rest of the tribe. It was a wharè Pakeha, built by Henere in right of the admixture of English blood in his veins, and not, I truly believe, from any preference for that style of building over the old Maori kind.

There was no one about when I arrived, so I walked through the two rooms and out at the back. The rooms were furnished with a few tables and chairs and other things, much after the style of married settlers in a small way. Out behind the house was an open space, where a fire was burning, with a billy boiling upon it. Close to the fire, superintending the cooking, her hair hanging in elf-locks round her head and over her face, squatting on the ground with her chin on her knees, a pipe in her mouth, and a dirty blanket over her shoulders as her only garment, was Mrs. Tangiao, the lady of the riding-habit.

Naturally, you would suppose that such an elegant and civilized young bride would blush with shame and dismay at being discovered by me in such utter *déshabillé*. Not a bit of it! Up she jumped, all smiles and welcomes, her blanket falling off as she did so, and leaving her as naked as a mahogany Venus. Even this did not discompose her in the least, as she warmly shook hands with me, and with truly childlike innocence offered her lips for a fraternal salute.

But the most comical part of the whole affair is yet to be told. A hearty coo-ee or two brought up Henere, who was at work in his cultivation at no great distance. After he had shaken me by the hand and warmly welcomed me, he began to scold the unlucky Mata. Not on the score of indelicacy or indecency, though; no such thought as that crossed his brain, good easy man! He only reproved his wife for not showing sufficient and proper honour to her "rangatira Pakeha" guest, which could not be done, he considered, unless she were completely attired in full Pakeha costume.

So, while I sat on the verandah and sipped some tea, Henere commenced to dress up his bride before my very eyes. He put on and fastened every article of her best clothes, combed and brushed out her redundant hair, decked and ornamented her with all the ribbons and laces and so on of which her wardrobe could boast. Meanwhile, the lady remained quite passive under his hands, sitting or standing or turning about as required, but all the while with serious unmoved expression of face, and puckered-up lips. Her large wondering eyes she kept fixed intently upon me, to note the effect the processes of her toilette were having upon me. I was very nearly strangled with suppressed laughter, but it would have mortally offended these simple, earnest people to have shown the least sense of the ridiculous.

When all was finished, and Mrs. Tangiao was costumed in English fashion, and very nicely, too, let me say, her husband made her enter the sitting-room and sit down upon a chair. Then he turned to me, unbounded satisfaction visible in his beaming face, inflated breast, and gesturing hands.

"You come see common Maori, sah? You come find Pakeha gentleman, Pakeha lady, Pakeha house! Good, good! Now you sit talk to my missee, I get Pakeha dinner."

After the meal we took a stroll through the kainga, Mata trying to attitudinize after the fashion of the white ladies she had seen in the settlements; and Henere loftily informing his neighbours that "*We three Pakeha* come to see *your* Maori town" —a piece of humour that was thoroughly enjoyed by both men and women, who made great capital for numberless jokes out of it.

CHAPTER V.

MAORI MANNERS.

III.

HALF-BREEDS, or Anglo-Maori men and women, form no inconsiderable section of the native community. Some have said of them, that they inherit the vices of both their parents, and the virtues of neither, but I cannot say that my own observation goes to support such a sweeping allegation. I have had some good friends among the Anglo-Maori, and never noticed any predominant vice in their character at all.

In complexion and general appearance, the Anglo-Maori resemble Spaniards or Italians, though they possess more or less marked traits of either the English or the Maori blood that mixes in their veins. Their physique is usually good, though they incline to slenderness and delicacy. They are by no means to be stigmatized as idle, but their capacity for work seems less than that of either parent. They lack the shrewdness of the Maori, and have not the mental power of the Anglo-Saxon. When a half-breed is bad, he seems to be wholly so, without any redeeming good qualities.

The Anglo-Maori women are nearly all very graceful and good-looking. There are some among them that are only to be described in the strongest language, as exceedingly beautiful. I have met a voluptuous beauty of this mixed race, an educated and fashionable lady, whose rare and exquisite loveliness might have made her the cause and heroine of another Trojan war. Once I knew one who possessed the most magnificent hair I ever expect to see.

We were playing croquet, I remember, some half a dozen people. The ladies had been bathing, I think; at any rate, they wore their hair flowing loose. I never saw anything like it. She, my partner in the game, had a complete mantle of dark-brown silky tresses. Her hair fell in volumes round her, and actually trailed on the ground when she stood upright. What an advertisement she would have been for a "hair-restorer!"

You know that at croquet one sometimes kneels to place the balls at a lady's feet, in order that she may have them in proper position for striking. That envious wind! It would blow my partner's beautiful long hair about. And, when performing that kneeling operation, the hair *would* come fluttering about one, and getting entangled round one's neck somehow. And then, dark tender eyes would look down with a sweep of velvety lashes, and gaze mockingly through the silky meshes of unruly floating hair, and one would be asked in caressing tones—

" Oh, dear! I'm afraid I've caught you! Have I, really ? "

That game was a dreadfully embarrassing one, yet quite too delicious and delightfully utter.

Anglo-Maori may be said to be divided into two distinct classes—those whose education has been chiefly or altogether English, and those who have "tumbled up" in the kainga, in all respects like Maori. The first are very much the fewest. A small number have been thoroughly well educated, perhaps in Sydney or in England, and are in all respects ladies and gentlemen of the English pattern. Some of these ladies have married well, into the best Australian or English society. I am told that two or three have even secured titles. Their beauty and sprightliness would cause them to be an ornament to any society. But the bulk of the Anglo-Maori are more like my friend Henere Tangiao, not appreciably different from the pure Maori among whom their lot is cast, save in a more Caucasian physique and a lighter complexion.

Intermarriage between the races is generally considered to be a very good and desirable thing by the Maori. Not that they hold themselves in any degree inferior to the Pakeha, or think a Maori girl elevated by wedding one; but they are aware of their own coming extinction as a race, and they think that intermarriage might serve to perpetuate Maori blood. It will be remembered that our native neighbours in the Kaipara are strongly inclined to this view.

Settlers look upon mixed marriages with different feelings. I think that most of us are in favour of them theoretically, but perhaps a less number care to regard them from a nearer point of view. There are some, of course, who are violently opposed to them in any case. But there is here none of that *caste* feeling which prevails in India against the Eurasians, or in America and the West Indies against negro admixture.

Nearly all such alliances have been between Pakeha men and Maori women. There have been instances of Englishwomen marrying men of the other race, but they have been very rare, nor do I recollect any such case myself. An Englishwoman, even of the lowest class, would find it difficult to reconcile herself to the life of the wharè and to the abject servitude, which is the lot of even the helpmate of an ariki. The condition in which they keep their wives is even yet little better than it used to be in former days. Moreover, there would always be the fear of polygamy.

Polygamy is not often met with now among the Maori, yet it is not entirely extinct, though it has become somewhat unofficial in kind. The missionaries set their faces against it from the very first, and made the putting away of his superfluous wives the condition of a convert's acceptance for baptism. They seem, indeed, to have carried their opposition to polygamy to rather too great a length, forgetting that a new phase of thought, when it operates practically, should be a gradual growth, if its effect is to be deep and permanent.

Under the first strong influence of conversion the Maori readily gave in to missionary insistance in this matter; but after awhile the old habit reconquered them. Then came individual relapses into barbarism, individual antagonism with the missionaries, and much division and heart-burning. It would have been better, in my humble opinion, to have ignored polygamy, or at least not to have pointed at it so particularly. It would have been better to have allowed things to remain as they were, in this respect, and to have relied on bringing up the young generations to the Christian observance of matrimony. Indeed, some few missionaries did adopt a line of action something like this, and found it the wisest in the long run.

By-and-by, the Maori began to seriously argue the matter. They took their Bibles, which they had been taught to regard as the standard of right and wrong, and asked the missionaries to show them where polygamy was forbidden. Nay, was it not divinely sanctioned in many parts of the Old Testament?

The Maori is naturally an acute reasoner and casuist, and those missionaries who stood out so emphatically against polygamy now found themselves worsted on their own ground. The arguments that have prevailed throughout Christendom in favour of monogamy were not accepted by the Maori. They wanted direct Biblical ordinance, and as that was not forthcoming they assumed that polygamy was lawful, or, at least, some of them chose to do so. Then there was great joy. There were marriages and giving in marriage, after the good old custom. Probably, this controversy on the matrimonial question was one of the causes that afterwards eventuated in Hau-hau.

In these days polygamy is very rare, chiefly

because the men outnumber the women, and because Maori find it expedient to conform to Pakeha custom. I visited a hapu once, whose chief had three wives; but he was an earnest Christian—*à la Maori*. He held prayers morning and evening in front of his wharè, at which all the people of the kainga attended. He conducted a long and lugubrious service every Sunday, expounding the Scriptures and preaching like a Spurgeon. He kept the Sabbath rigidly sacred, and interlarded his conversation with texts. Altogether he was a model man, never getting drunk except when he visited the township, never cheating anybody unless he was doing business with him.

Bonâ-fide marriages between white men and Maori women are seldomer contracted now than they used to be. I knew a man whose Maori bride brought him ten thousand acres of rich land as a dowry. She was a delicious little brown innocent, just such another as Mrs. Tangiao. Another man I knew married a Maori girl out of gratitude, she having saved his life from her own people in the early warlike days. She had acted towards him in a similar way to that in which Rahab of Jericho did to the Hebrew spies.

Alliances of a less enduring kind than these are matters of not infrequent occurrence. I have hinted at the hospitable customs of the primitive kainga, and the peculiar freedom, in certain respects, of unmarried Maori girls. It is not necessary to say any more on that head, I think. In justice to the race, it is only fair to say, that no more faithful or virtuous *wife* exists than a Maori one. Derelictions of conjugal duty both were and are very rarely known, in spite of somewhat arbitrary match-making. Such are a heinous crime in Maori eyes.

There are certain drawbacks that are apt to mar the conjugal felicity of the Pakeha who weds a Maori. He is received as a member of the hapu from which he has selected his bride, and is looked upon by all Maori as being in a closer relationship to them than other Pakeha. This adds other inconveniences to those arising from your wife's predilection for squatting on the drawing-room floor and smoking her pipe; her careless *negligé* in dress, except on state occasions; and her many little delightful and eccentric propensities. For, you have married not only your wife, but also all her relations and kindred.

They will visit you, twenty or thirty at a time, and stop a week or longer. They will slaughter your pigs and sheep, dig up your potatoes and kumera, and feed freely upon them. Your grocery bill will attain to frightful proportions; and the friendly mob will camp all over the house, just how and where it pleases them. If you resent these proceedings, your wife will cry and upbraid you, and might even desert you altogether, while the hapu would look upon it as the deadliest insult. As a *per contra*, your wife's tribe will stand by you in all difficulties and dangers. They will fight for you with pleasure, will die for you and with you if required; and a slight put upon you by anybody whatsoever, is put upon the tribe in equal degree.

You may cajole these ladies and gentlemen into helping you with any work that is going forward, but the perquisites they will take to themselves will be safe to ruin you. You may return their visits, as much as you like, but that will not reimburse you much. All that remains to you to do is to sell your land, and to remove to some distant part of the country, where there are no Maori. You must, in such a case, carefully prepare some artful and specious tale to satisfy your numerous relations-in-law, and mitigate their grief at losing you. Lastly, you must not take your wife out of New Zealand, for she will pine, and possibly die, if you do.

Although the old Maori are commonly spoken of as savages, they certainly did possess a degree of civilization of their own. They had a traditional history, a well-defined mythology, a code of laws based on the tapu, a perfect tribal organization, industries and arts of no mean kind. Among them were men, renowned long after their death in song and story, as great statesmen, warriors, poets, artists, and so on. Their dwellings are of simple construction, but they are superior to Irish cabins by a long way. Many of them were extravagantly decorated with carvings and ornaments. The fortified pa were planned with surprising engineering skill, and could be defended against English troops. Even where artillery was brought against the pa, the earthworks made the siege no light work. Sometimes our troops were actually repulsed from before these forts, as at Ohaeawae and Okaehau.

The Maori cultivations were often extensive, though, before the coming of Captain Cook, the articles cultivated were not of great variety. Taro, the farinaceous bulb of an arum; Kumera, the tuber of a species of convolvulus; and Hue, the calabash or gourd, were the crops; to which Cook and those who came after him added potatoes, maize, wheat, oats and barley, turnips, cabbages, peas, beans, fruit-trees, and many other things, which were sedulously grown and spread among their tribes by the Maori.

In many ways the Maori proved their patient and careful industry. They made for themselves tools of all kinds—axes, adzes, chisels, knives—out of flint and jade, shells and shark's-teeth; and they also contrived various formidable weapons. Many of these articles are accurately curved and shaped, polished and carved. With tools of this nature the Maori levelled the gigantic kauri pine, and cut from its trunk the ponderous waka-taua, or war-canoe; cut and shaped with an accuracy that would stand the test of nice geometrical instruments.

The war-canoes were fitted with richly carved prows, stern-posts, and side-pieces, often inlaid with shells and greenstone. They were sixty or seventy feet in length; and would hold over a hundred men. With forty or fifty paddles on a side, one of these canoes could be driven through the water with all the velocity of a steam-ram or racing skiff.

Not only canoes, but also the fronts of dwelling and council-houses were adorned with elaborate workmanship. Then there was a kind of wooden statuary, which was set up in kainga and wahi-tapu; and there were picture-writings cut upon rocks and trees. Weapons, tools, personal ornaments, tiki—or image-amulets—and so forth, showed very great care and cleverness in design. The ornamentation was very intricate, was finished off with surprising nicety, and was executed in a style that cannot but excite our wonder. For, it is to be recollected, that the Maori possessed no metal tools or instruments.

Grotesque and curious as is Maori sculpture, it

yet clearly evidences some artistic leanings. There was doubtless some sort of Society of Arts among the tribes. For, certain men or women, peculiarly skillful in some special particular, became persons of great renown throughout the land, and their services were sought after by favour, force, and fraud.

The highest branch of art, or, at least, what was esteemed to be such, was the Maori heraldry, and its emblazonment upon the living skin. Artists skilled in this making of the moku—tattooers, as we Pakeha call them—were tremendous dignitaries. Their talents were a gift, were held to be genius, and no means were hesitated at which could secure one of these persons to a tribe. Battles were fought for them, and poetical biographies of some of them are even yet current. Such was the Art-cultus of the Maori.

In pursuing the subject of ancient Maori civilization, there are many points worthy of note. Dress is one of these. Although the Maori were accustomed to walk about completely naked—save and except the moku on their face, chest, and thighs—yet they had garments that were always donned on state occasions, at night, and when the weather was cold.

Of course they had no idea of indecency, and, indeed, have only a forced and artificial sense of it now. Naked as they were in person, they were still more natural in mind, and this quality is still notably apparent. It is not possible for a Maori to talk for five minutes without uttering words, metaphors, and allusions, that to us convey the most revolting and shocking notions, though the speaker is entirely unconscious of anything but the simplest matter of fact. The language, as colloquially used, is full of stumbling blocks to English refinement, and it is for this reason, doubtless, that few settlers' wives and daughters learn it at all, even though they may be living in the midst of Maori.

The garments of the Maori consisted of a breechclout and a toga, made principally from phormium fibre. I have called the chief universal garment a *toga*, instead of giving it the ordinary designation of " mat," or " blanket," because it was worn after the manner of the old Roman toga; and, though a heavy, bundling kind of dress, it gave a certain sort of dignity to the wearer. These two articles were all the garments proper, but several ornaments were added to them. A kind of helmet was occasionally worn; and sandals were used by persons with delicate feet, when walking over rough ground.

The mats were made in considerable variety, of dog-skins, and of flax-fibre. Some were very elaborate and adorned with fringes, tassels, and embroidery, being dyed of various colours. Some, made from a choice species of phormium, were soft and silky. Into the threads of others were woven feathers of the kiwi and other birds. These two last kinds were highly prized.

The whole process of making the simplest of these dresses shows a degree of patient, industrial enterprise, highly creditable to the operators. First of all, the flax (*Phormium tenax*) was gathered, dried, macerated, beaten, and the fibre picked out with the fingers, combed, bleached, and otherwise prepared. By these arduous and laborious processes it was entirely freed from the gum which permeates the leaf, and could be wound into thread of various degrees of fineness. That accomplished, it was woven into cloth, upon a frame of wooden pins stuck into the ground. Fringes and embroidery were manufactured with the simplest possible appliances, and the juice of sundry trees, plants, and berries, yielded good dyes of different hues.

The kaitaka, a toga with a silky gloss and texture, was very highly esteemed; but a still rarer and most valuable garment was the Weweru mo te huru kiwi, or toga of kiwi's feathers. This was an ample robe of woven flax, upon the outside of which were the feathers. Now, as each feather of the kiwi is about two or three inches long, and only a line or so in breadth—more like a coarse hair than any other feather, in fact—and as each feather was separately worked into the texture of the flax, and as these feathers were so plentifully disposed upon the mat as to give it the appearance of thick fur, some idea may be gained of the prodigious labour involved in making such a toga, from first to last.

The commonest and coarsest mat took a woman six months to make; the kaitaka took much longer; while the feather robe occupied the exclusive time of several women for a period of two or three years. But then, it was a grand property, lasting not only a lifetime, but capable of being handed down from generation to generation. It was quite impervious to rain or wind, and though somewhat bulky, was of light weight. Besides these, a chief prized his robe of long-haired white and yellow dogskins.

There was another kind of closely-woven dress, te pukaha, which served as defensive armour against javelins and lances, before the introduction of muskets. There were various differences of make, indicating a species of sumptuary law; but all the dresses, of men and women, of chiefs and slaves, had the same common characteristics.

The Maori neither are nor were at any time pinched for food. An erroneous impression has gone abroad that their cannibalism was the result of a lack of anything else to eat. This is a totally wrong idea, as I had occasion to point out in a former chapter, when speaking as to the causes which are bringing about the extinction of the race. The act of cannibalism was a part of the system of warfare; it was the last outrage upon an always detested foeman; the utmost indignity that revenge could heap upon the enemy. Although, in the earlier part of this century, no less than fifteen hundred prisoners of war were killed and eaten at a single feast by Hongi and his army, and six hundred on another occasion, yet the last authenticated act of cannibalism took place in 1843; and, nowadays, Maori rather avoid allusion to the subject. But it was only the prisoners of war who were eaten, and that usually just after the battle, before the heat and intoxication of the conquerors' spirits had evaporated. They never ate human flesh at other times, and prisoners whose lives were spared became slaves—an easy kind of slavery it was, too.

In the primitive times, should the crops of a hapu fail them, or become too soon exhausted, there was always fish in the rivers and fern-root in the valleys, so that, however "hard up" a man might be, he would not need to starve very long. Though the moa was probably very scarce, if not entirely extinct, towards the beginning of this century, yet the bush abounded with birds that the Maori knew well how to catch. Pigeons, nestors, parrots, rail, kiwi, swamp-fowl, water-fowl, owls, parson-birds, all these and more were eaten; while the native dogs and rats were held to be great dainties. The former were bred in numbers, and were fattened up for food, and their skins were highly valued for togas and mantles. An elaborate code of ceremonies, songs, and customs are connected with rat-hunting, showing that rats were so numerous as to be no inconsiderable part of the food supply.

Then there were certain grubs and insects that were held to be delicate morsels. The loathsome larva of the weta, a large white grub, is speared on a stick, toasted at the fire, and eaten with a silent rapture that my pen could only feebly pourtray.

In the bays and tidal rivers are the mango or sharks—the most highly-prized food-fish—the tamure or schnapper, the whapuka or rock-cod, the kahawai or mackerel, the porahi or herring, the kanae or mullet, the patiki or sole, and many others. On the shores are oysters, mussels, cockles, mutton-fish, crabs, and other shell-fish in profuse abundance. In the fresh-water creeks are eels (tuna), lampreys (pipiharau), and whitebait (inanga).

Among indigenous vegetable productions came first the universal fern-root (*Pteris esculenta*), which was cooked in various ways and made into a kind of bread. Then there was the tap-root of the cabbage-tree palm, yielding a highly farinaceous food when baked; the pith or young shoot of the nikau; the root of the toi; the root of the raupo, and the pollen of the same plant made into bread; the berries of hinau, similarly treated; the flower and fruit of kiekie or tawhera; a species of seaweed boiled with the juice of tupakihi berries, and forming a nutritious jelly; some orchids, green spinach, cresses, and fungi; the inner stems of mamaku or tree-fern; the berries of poroporo, tawa-tawa, koraka, kahikatea, rimu, and other trees.

The expressed juice of the tupakihi berry is called by the Maori tutu. It is a pleasantly insipid drink when fresh made, but appears to undergo a slight fermentation when allowed to stand some time, and when mixed with some other ingredient. The seeds are always carefully eliminated from this preparation, as they contain a dangerous narcotic principle. The old Maori say, that in ancient times, before going into battle, they used to eat taro to make them strong and enduring, shark-meat to make them ferocious, and used to drink tutu to make them brave and unflinching.

The Maori cooking operations were, in former times, always performed by women and slaves;

now, though women are invariably the cooks in the kainga, yet no man considers it beneath him to prepare his own food when obliged to do so. Most of the old methods of cooking have fallen very much into disuse, since the modern Maori possess kettles, iron camp-ovens, billies, and other Pakeha appliances; but still, in remote spots, one may come across a relic of the olden time.

The only method of boiling formerly employed was by dropping heated stones into the water contained in a calabash or rind of the hue. Expert as they were in this process, it was still a rather toilsome and ineffective one, and in these days of kettles and pans it is never returned to. Fish and meat were frequently roasted on the clear side of the fire in the ordinary hunters' fashion, but the great national culinary institution was the earth-oven, the kopa or hangi.

A pit was dug in the ground, one foot or more in depth, and suited in size to the quantity of provisions to be cooked. In this hole a fire was built, completely filling it, and in the fire a number of pebble stones were heated. When the fire had reached a proper heat it was entirely raked out of the pit. A layer of the red-hot stones was laid along the bottom, by means of improvised tongs of green wood, and these were carefully and quickly covered with certain green leaves. Then the pork or fish or potatoes, previously washed, cleaned, and wrapped up in green flax, were put into the hangi; a quantity of the red-hot stones were put over and round it; water was poured over the whole; green flax mats were hastily heaped on top and tucked in at the sides; and, lastly, the pit was filled in with earth well stamped and beaten down.

In the course of an hour or more, according to the size of the joint, the hangi was opened, the provisions lifted out, the wrappings unfolded, and their contents placed in baskets of green flax, and thus dinner was served. The steam, generated under pressure in the ovens, was forced into every fibre of the articles cooking, so that these were most thoroughly done. Whole pigs—and whole human bodies in the cannibal times—are cooked in these hangi to perfection. I have eaten meat and vegetables done in them, that could not have been better cooked by a *chef de cuisine* decorated with the red ribbon of *la Légion d'honneur*.

It was one of the old customs never to eat in the living-houses. Cooking was always performed in the open air, and usually is so still. A rude shelter protected the fire in rainy weather; and at such times the meal was eaten under the verandah of the tharè.

Burial customs among the old Maori were peculiar and complicated, and differed much among various hapu. In the case of slaves and inferiors, the bodies were thrown aside in some place where they could not be offensive to the living, or they were hastily interred on the beach, or somewhere in the forest.

The death of a chief, or rangatira of note, was an affair of great importance. It was announced by loud wailing and crying—the Maori idea of grief being a noisy and demonstrative one. The corpse was washed and painted, dressed in the finest garments and ornaments possessed by the defunct, and laid in state in the verandah of the wharè, with a great display of weapons and trophies of various kinds around it. All the near relations of the deceased assembled to cry over him, and many—particularly of the ladies of his family—gashed their faces, breasts, and arms, with shells and obsidian knives. It was thought to be the most decorous and decent show of mourning to have the face and breast completely covered with the dried and clotted blood resulting from the numerous self-inflicted gashes.

After a day or two of these ceremonies, the body was taken by the tohunga and his assistants within the sacred grove, or wahi tapu. There, still wrapped in his most cherished robes, with all his ornaments, weapons, and ensigns of dignity around him, with baskets of food to support him on his journey to the other world—and, in olden times, with a strangled wife and slave or two—the corpse was left, either placed in the fork of a tree, on an ornamental platform or stage, or buried in the ground.

Meanwhile, during the progress of these ceremonies, many karakia, or prayers, were uttered; and the multitude of friends, relations, and followers assembled outside the wahi tapu made the air resound with their frantic shouts and yells, with the firing of guns, and every possible kind of noise. When the body had been thus deposited and left, a great feast took place, something after the manner of an Irish wake.

In the course of a couple of years or so after, when the tohunga deemed that decomposition was complete, a second series of ceremonies took place. This was called the hahunga, or scraping of the bones. Amid renewed wailing and weeping from the assembled friends, the bones of the dead were collected by the tohunga. They were scraped clean with a good deal of ceremony and karakia, were painted, garnished with feathers, wrapped up in rich mats, and abundantly wept over. Finally, they were deposited high up in some sacred tree, or in a fissure of the rock, or upon an elevated stage profusely ornamented, and then they were done with.

Many burying-places still exist, filled with these weird mementoes of the past. Of course no Maori, however Christianized or civilized he may be, will knowingly trespass within their limits; but Pakeha do so frequently. Collectors of "curios" have found in these places a rich field for treasure-seeking; but, even at the present day, and among the most law-abiding tribes, it is by no means safe to go curio-hunting in the old and apparently forgotten wahi tapu. The Maori are intensely averse from allowing any stranger to penetrate these places, and if they caught any one despoiling their dead, it would rouse a flame among them not easily to be appeased. Certain lands upon which are situated such sacred spots are not to be bought for love or money from their Maori owners. Still, as the rising generation steps into the shoes of its fathers, prejudices of this kind give way before the influence of Pakeha gold.

Some land, in a settled district that I know well, was much sought after a year or two ago by persons settling in the neighbourhood, it being of particularly choice quality; but the central part of this block being a burial-place, the old chief, who was the principal owner, refused large offers, and would not part with an acre of the sacred soil for any inducement that could be held out to him. Lately, however, he died, and his young heirs were persuaded—not without much difficulty, though—to sell the block to an English settler.

Nowadays, the burial of a man of rank is conducted upon different principles. I witnessed the interment of a lady of high rank among the Ngapuhi, at Waimate, which may serve to illustrate modern customs in this respect. The deceased, though externally differing but little from the usual dirty, repulsive-looking, and hag-like appearance of old Maori women, was yet a personage of great note and consequence. She was the last lineal descendant of a great chief, and possessed all the authority of a queen or princess-absolute herself. Consequently, when she died, the hapu—or section of the tribe—of which she was the undisputed head resolved to celebrate the occasion with the most gorgeous obsequies it was in their power to get up.

The body was laid in state and wailed over, but there was not much cutting of faces done, only a sort of compromise between the old custom and the usages of a more enlightened age—a scratch or two here and there, made by the most conservative among the mourners. A coffin was made, or procured, and a rich pall of black velvet and white silk covered it. The procession then set out for Waimate, distant some eight or ten miles from the deceased's kainga.

The coffin was borne on a litter between two horses, and the procession was formed by several hundred mounted Maori, of both sexes and all ages, all dressed in their best attire, some with crape scarves, but mostly without. They proceeded in a long straggling line, the coffin being borne along in front, and in that manner wound over the ranges and through the bush towards the settlement and mission-church of Waimate.

At times there was much cheerful laughter and talking in the procession, and parties would suddenly dash out of the ranks for a furious gallop. Then there would be a mournful wave pass over the cavalcade, and long-drawn wails and cries of sorrow would break forth from all. This again would alternate with sudden gaiety ; and so, in such manner, the churchyard was reached. The horses were tethered all round the churchyard fence, and their riders, augmented by a crowd of others who had assembled on foot, and by the whole population of the settlement, entered the church.

The service was conducted in the ordinary manner of the Church of England. But when the coffin was lowered into the grave, the Maori who crowded round it appeared heart-broken with grief. Tears streamed down every face, eyes were turned up to heaven, while sobs and moans and clamorous wailing broke out on all sides.

A few minutes after the service was completed the sorrowing crowd dispersed, all hastening in the direction of the village where the funeral feast was to be held. Many of the cavaliers started off with loud whoops, upon an exciting race at the utmost speed of their horses, while all banished, for the time being, every semblance of grief.

I went to the kainga in the evening, as unobtrusively as possible, to see how the feasting was conducted. Men and women sat, stood, lay, or lounged about, clustering round the fires and ovens every now and then to do some feeding, or laughing, chatting, smoking, and generally enjoying themselves. But, every now and then, some one would set up a loudly-chanted lament, and instantly all would crouch upon the ground in a sitting posture, and, while the tears fell in abundance from their eyes, would wail and rock themselves about in the most terrible anguish of grief, apparently. In a minute or two this would subside, and all would return at once, and without an effort, to their former cheerfulness.

O'Gaygun, who had accompanied me, said that

if there had only been a fiddler present, to play *The Coina* or *Savournah Deelish*, the resemblance to a wake in "ould Oireland" would have been complete; for "lashins of whiskey was goin', annyhow!"

In this manner several days and nights were spent. I am afraid to say how many sheep and pigs were killed, how many tons of potato and kumera, and sacks of flour, were devoured; but the total, I know, was something prodigious. The stores at Ohaeawae and Waitangi did a roaring trade in supplying tea, sugar, tobacco, liquor, and the other requirements of the feasters.

There was a very singular custom prevalent among the Maori called the *moru*. If a misfortune of any kind happened to a man, all his neighbours, headed by his nearest and dearest friends, instantly came down upon him and pillaged him of everything he possessed.

In 1827, Mr. Earle, who resided some time in New Zealand, and afterwards published a narrative of his experiences, relates that the houses or huts belonging to himself and his companions on Kororareka Beach accidentally caught fire. The fire took place at a rather critical moment, just when a number of Maori had arrived to do battle with the Kororareka natives, who were Earle's allies. Directly the fire broke out, both parties suspended preparations for hostilities and rushed upon the devoted little settlement, which they pillaged of everything that could be carried off. Earle and his party could do nothing to prevent them, and they were thus stripped of the greater part of their possessions, according to the custom of the moru.

A peculiarity of the Maori race is the singular power that imagination has over them. It seems, indeed, to take practical effect, and the suddenness with which the will can operate is not less startling than the action so induced.

A Maori can throw himself into a transport of rage, grief, joy, or fear, at a moment's notice. This is not acting either, it is grim reality, as many an instance proves. For example, there is Hau-hau. The principal manifestation in that singular new religion is the ecstasy and excitement into which whole congregations appear to throw themselves. There is something akin to the mesmeric phenomena in the extraordinary gusts of feeling that sweep over a Hau-hau conventicle. The leader works himself up first, and then the rest follow. They shout, they scream, they roll on the ground, they weep, they groan, and, while in this state, appear insensible to every external influence but the strange excitement that possesses them.

Any Maori can die when he likes. He wills it,

and the fact is accomplished. He says, perhaps, "I am going to die on Wednesday next!" and when the day comes, he really goes into the bush, lays down and expires.

Then they can weep at will. A tangi (weeping) can be performed by any Maori at a moment's notice. Though they are a cheerful and laughter-loving people, they make the tangi a frequent ceremony. A Maori will be laughing and talking in the greatest glee and high spirits, when he is suddenly accosted by a friend of his whom he may not have seen for some time. Instantly the two will crouch upon the ground with faces close together, and, rocking their bodies from side to side, wailing and sobbing, the tears will drop from their eyes and roll down their cheeks more abundantly than most Britons would think possible; like a shower of summer rain, in fact.

This is the ordinary mode of recognition of friends, founded, no doubt, upon the insecurity of life that formerly prevailed. Partings are effected in the same way; and on all occasions where grief is really felt, or where it is considered necessary or in accordance with etiquette to put on the semblance of grief, a tangi takes place.

Modern usage, however, following even more closely in the European style with every succeeding generation, has rather spoilt this among other customs. That is to say, most young Maori of the period do not tangi unless they are really affected with the emotion of grief, although they do not seem to have lost the power of weeping at will.

One of our neighbours, who had formed a close intimacy with the Maori of the district, went home on a visit to England. We heard that he intended to return in the ill-fated ship *Cospatrick*, and when the news arrived of the terrible disaster which overtook that vessel, we mourned our friend as among the lost.

A party of his Maori friends arrived at his farm, and held there a sort of combined tangi and prayer-meeting. When he finally turned up, having luckily come out in another ship, the Maori assembled from all sides, and so warmly did they congratulate him on his safety, that they were obliged to hold another tangi to give proper effect to their feelings. Though there may seem to be something childlike and pleasing about this custom theoretically, I cannot say that it is particularly agreeable in practice or to participate in.

The old Maori method of salutation was to press the noses together. Like many more old customs, it is now nearly quite forgotten; the Pakeha hand-shaking and the Pakeha kissing having altogether superseded it. Only once was I subjected to the nose-pressing process, which was done to me by a very old rangatira,—our very good friend the Rev. Tama-te-Whiti, in fact—who took that means of showing a more than ordinary esteem for me on a certain occasion elsewhere spoken of.

In these days the Maori no longer manufacture any of their old tools, weapons, ornaments, clothes, etc. They now buy Pakeha goods at the stores, and prefer them to their old appliances; in fact, the latter are becoming very scarce, since the bulk of them are eagerly bought up by collectors as " curios." Very few of the waka-taua, or war-canoes, are now in native possession, though, until recently, there used to be a race of them at the Auckland regatta on Anniversary Day (January 29.)

The various sorts of ordinary canoes are still plentiful enough, though they are probably destined to disappear before very long. The Maori do not make them now, they build or purchase boats made after the Pakeha fashion. The old canoe is an ungainly and uncomfortable vessel, hollowed out of the trunk of a single tree. It rides flat on the water, and is very seaworthy, being with difficulty upset, and going as well when full of water as when dry. The canoes are driven by slender spear-shaped paddles, that are dug into the water, as it were; with them a great speed can be attained, nevertheless. The ordinary canoes will carry from a dozen to a score of persons; but some are larger, like the war-canoes, and would hold a hundred or more, pretty tightly packed, though.

The race at the Auckland regatta used to be an exciting sight. The canoes, with their high, carved prows and stern-posts, were richly decorated with all sorts of barbaric ornaments. (It was only the waka-taua that were so furnished, ordinary canoes not having prows, stern-posts, or bulwarks attached to them.) They were crammed with rowers, chosen from among the strongest men of the contesting hapu. At the stern, upon a sort of deck, stood the chief, costumed in his bravest robes and ornaments, and carrying a patu, truncheon, or long wand in his hand.

The race would start with boat-chaunts among the paddlers, gradually enlivened by jibing shouts at the rival canoes. Then, as the race grew hotter, the foam would begin to fly as the paddles dashed up the water; the chiefs would stamp and rage on their platforms, shouting encouragement to their own men and yelling defiance to the others. When the termination of the race drew near, the yells and screams would be deafening, the energy of the paddlers exerted to the utmost, the gesticulations and cries of the chiefs only to be compared to those of frenzied madmen, and the excitement and fury of all concerned would seem only to be ended in bloodshed.

But all this excitement would quiet down after the goal was won, and no fighting or ill-feeling was the consequence. Nowadays, at the various regattas held on the rivers at different times, craft of all kinds, owned and manned by Maori, will amicably contest with those of settlers; and, whether in the whaleboat or the skiff, the Maori are formidable opponents to the Pakeha, who by no means invariably snatch the prize.

In common with the disappearance of the canoe is that of many other articles of native manufacture. Their old tools and weapons are rarities even among themselves, having long ago been bartered away for the more useful instruments of the Pakeha; and the art of making them has been forgotten. Even the almost sacred merè ponamu is a thing of the past. It was a large axe formed of "greenstone," or transparent green jade, often exquisitely shaped and polished. It was sometimes mounted on an elaborate handle, much carved and ornamented; or, in most cases, it was shaped in the short club-like form of the favourite weapon, all in one piece, and adapted for one hand.

The merè ponamu was the special weapon of the ariki, and was emblematic of his dignity. A good deal of sanctity attached to it, and it was held to be a tribal treasure. When defeated or threatened with its loss, the ariki or tohunga would hide the merè; and often the hiding-place would be unknown, since the chief might be killed before he could reveal it to his successor. In such a case the most careful and painstaking search would be afterwards entered upon by the tribe, who would even continue it for years, until the treasure was discovered.

It will be remembered how Tuwharè hid the tiki of the Ngatewhatua, after the capture of Marahemo by Hongi. A tiki is a grotesque image, carved out of the same stone—ponamu—as the merè. Much the same degree of sanctity attached to either. Merè made of wood, bone, or other kinds of stone had, of course, no especial value. When a new ariki was called to lead the tribe, he was invested with the merè ponamu with much important ceremony, just as Turkish sultans are girded with the sword of Othman, in token of their assumption of supreme power.

Not many years ago, it chanced that a gumdigger accidentally found a merè ponamu in the bush. The first person he happened to meet was a Maori, to whom he showed his "find." The

Maori examined it carefully, and questioned the digger as to the precise locality in which he had found it. He then asked the digger to sell it to him, which, after some demur, the latter eventually consented to do, the price he put on the "curio" being three notes (£3). The Maori went off to fetch the money; and by-and-by returned to the digger's camp with one or two of his compatriots. The sale was then concluded, and after the Pakeha had expressed himself as satisfied with the bargain, he was somewhat chagrined at being told that the merè was the long-lost weapon of a great chief, which had been unsuccessfully searched for during long years, and that, had he demanded three hundred pounds instead of only three, the tribe would have found means to raise it, so much did they prize the relic.

It speaks highly for the sense of justice and peaceableness of the modern Maori that no thought of forcibly taking possession of the merè seems to have occurred to these men, although the digger was alone, and they were numerous. How different might the climax have been had they been Irish peasants instead of semi-civilized Maori!

The Maori have no sense of honour, but they have a keen love of justice, which suffices to take its place. Manifestations of their principles of equity are often very amusing to us; but they might sometimes serve to improve the decisions of our law-courts, despite their crudity. They are generally based on the idea of utu, or compensation, and are deliciously simple. Thus, adultery is now punished among the Maori themselves in the following fashion:—

The chiefs hold a korero, or palaver, over the offenders, and settle the amount of utu to be paid. The man has to pay a fine to the husband, father, or nearest relative of the woman; she, in like manner, is sentenced to pay a similar sum to the wife, mother, or nearest relative of the man. If a culprit has no property, he or she has to go towork among the Pakeha, or dig gum, or raise it in some such fashion. There never seems to be any attempt to evade a fine of this kind; it is always faithfully paid to the last penny.

A Maori stole a bag of sugar from a store. He was pulled up before the local magistrate, and sent for a month's imprisonment. When the term expired and he returned to the tribe, the chiefs held a korero over him as usual. To their ideas of equity, the imprisonment counted for nothing, it was simply one of the stupid Pakeha customs, and had merely delayed the course of real (Maori) justice. Accordingly, the thief was sentenced to pay the value of the stolen sugar to the proprietor of the store. Next, he had to pay utu to the same person; and, finally, he had to pay utu to the chiefs as representing the tribe, to compensate them for the loss of credit the community had sustained through his offence.

The following incident occurred in a district not otherwise alluded to in these sketches, and the locality of which is purposely concealed. Should it meet the eye of any person concerned, I beg he will hold me excused for recording it. It could only be identified by himself. I insert it simply because it is the best instance within my knowledge of Maori justice, and of modern Maori manners in this particular.

There were two brothers who had settled in a remote district. The elder of the two had occasion to go over to Sydney on business for some months, and left the younger to manage the farm in his absence. The young fellow had only a hired lad to bear him company, besides occasional visits from some of his chums among the neighbouring settlers. By-and-by the lad left him, and he hired a couple of Maori girls to do some of the necessary work.

I have described what Maori girls are like, and so, here, close intercourse very soon had its natural result, and human nature triumphed over Pakeha morality. The girls went back to their kainga after a time, and, after the wont of their race, made no secret of anything that had occurred.

Now the ariki of the little hapu had "got religion," as I have heard it phrased, and tried his best to be sanctimonious and pharisaic. He chose to affect violent rage on hearing of the young farmer's breach of Pakeha moral law, and sent off a demand for a large sum of money as utu, in default of payment of which he promised to come up and burn the farmer's house and drive off his stock.

The settler resented and repudiated this claim for utu altogether, and, hearing that the Maori were getting their guns ready for the raid, he summoned all his neighbours to assist in his defence. A dozen or more of them armed and came over to stop with him, and a very pretty little disturbance seemed imminent.

However, there was a clergyman who had great influence with the hapu. At first, he probably helped to kindle the chief's ire by inveighing against the hideous guilt of the farmer, after the manner of unworldly clerics; but, seeing subsequently the direction things were about to take, he altered his tactics. Knowing the Maori character thoroughly, he took what was certainly the best possible step under the circumstances.

Instead of preaching against war and bloodshed, he stopped the war-party, as it was setting off, by intimating that the house, land, and bulk of the stock belonged to the absent brother, and that it would, therefore, be wrong to touch it. Maori justice instantly perceived the point, and a korero was immediately held to discuss it. Then the chief and his advisers began to find themselves in a hopeless muddle. They could not withdraw the claim for utu honourably—according to their notions—and in default of it they must exact something. At the same time, it was repugnant to their ideas of justice to meddle with what belonged to an unoffending man, and he an absentee to boot. So the korero lasted day after day, and the Maori could find no way out of their dilemma.

Meanwhile, the father of the girl who had caused the mischief, and who was a greedy old wretch, happily cut the Gordian knot. While things were still unsettled, he sneaked off one day alone, and made his way to the farm. There he intimated to the young settler that he was prepared to take five notes for his daughter's wrong, and would consider all claims liquidated by it. The young man's blood was up, however, and he refused to pay the fraction of a penny as utu. But some of his friends were cooler; and after a long palaver the young fellow consented to purchase a horse from the Maori, at a price somewhat above its value.

Back went the outraged father to the hapu and told what he had done. The ariki scolded him heartily for his baseness, that is to say, for the small amount of utu he had exacted. But all were overjoyed at the incident, which served to make a way out of the difficulty. An ambassador was sent up to the farm with the following message from the ariki, which I roughly translate—

"Oh, friend! There is now peace, and things are smooth between us. Pita is a fool, he took what was too little. That is his affair, and I have told him my mind. You have made utu to him and the wretch is satisfied. That ends all. I have no more to say. We are friends as before."

And now arose a new phase of Maori character. They are always very desirous to get up alliances between the races, and will do anything to induce a Pakeha to marry a Maori girl. Even such informal engagements as that just hinted at are so far from being repugnant to them, that they generally show an increased regard for the Pakeha who is indiscreetly amorous among their *unmarried* women.

The chief in this case was governed, in the first instance, by an artificial veneer of sentiment inculcated by the new religion. Now that this was broken through, and the vexed question of utu disposed of, the genuine Maori feeling rose to the surface, and a warm friendliness arose for the Pakeha —the *rangatira* Pakeha be it remembered—who had shown that he "liked the Maori girls."

Accompanied by a score or so of the rangatira of his hapu, the ariki rode over to the young settler's place. As proof of the re-establishment of cordial relations, kitsful of peaches, melons, kumera, taro, and other gifts were carried by the party. The young man met them with all hospitality, killed a pig and feasted the party for a couple of days, presented a dog to the ariki, and finally paid a return visit to the kainga, where he was received with open arms by the entire hapu. He has ever since remained a prime favourite with the Maori, who, singularly enough, respected him for his line of action when the difficulty arose, almost as much as they warmed to him for his amorous predilection.

Little misunderstandings of this sort now and then arise between Pakeha and Maori, but they are generally smoothed down in some such fashion as the above. The worst difficulties are those where Maori of different tribes come into collision with one another, when the ancient feuds and hatreds spring up and cause much trouble. Especially is this the case when Christian sectarianism is an added element of bitterness and strife. I remember an instance of this that occurred in the north in 1875 or 1876.

There was a Land Court held in what was then quite a new district, and at it the chiefs of a Ngapuhi hapu laid claim to a certain block, which they had agreed to sell to a settler. But a Ngatewhatua, who was present by the merest chance, disputed the claim on the ground that the block formed a part of his tribal territory. The Ngapuhi ridiculed him, and replied that their tribe under Hongi had, in former times, conquered the Ngatewhatua and annexed their territory, leaving only a corner for the remnant of the conquered to live on. This was according to ancient Maori law.

But the Ngatewhatua declared that, also in accordance with Maori usage, the conquerors having never taken possession of the district nor resided on any part of the block, it reverted to its original owners, the Ngatewhatua. Both sides had thus a fair show of right, and neither having occupied the land within the memory of man, it was difficult to decide which had the best claim.

The commissioner left the Maori to come to some agreement among themselves, for he could not adjust their differences, while he was bound to find a native owner for the block before the Crown grant could be made out. Both sides now withdrew in great dudgeon, while the few Pakeha in the neighbourhood began to feel somewhat nervous and anxious as to what was to follow.

The Ngatewhatua returned to his hapu and related all that had occurred. A korero was immediately held and rapidly concluded. It was agreed at once that decisive action was necessary; so the ariki ordered his men to take their guns and other arms, to launch their boats, and proceed with him to the township where the Land Court was being held. All the available men of the hapu, some forty or fifty in number, were ready at the chief's command, and at once set off; while messages were sent to warn other communities of the Ngatewhatua, and to invite them to take part in the coming fray.

In due time, the ariki of the Ngatewhatua and his band arrived at the scene of action. They rowed up the river to the township where the Land Court was being held, and which was near the disputed block, with all the pomp and circumstance of Maori war, so far as it was possible in their modern civilized condition.

Near the little township, awaiting their arrival, was a still more numerous body of armed Ngapuhi, who greeted them with yells of defiance. The few officials and Pakeha at the place did their best to allay the excitement of the natives, but without success. They were not listened to, or were told to leave things alone. This was a purely Maori question, with which Pakeha had nothing to do; *they* were not in any way threatened; let them keep out of it, then.

But the settlers knew that this faction fight, if it once took place and resulted in bloodshed, might lead to a general conflagration among the northern tribes. They were at their wit's end to know what to do. It was no use sending to Auckland, for there were very few of the armed constabulary there; and, had there been more, they could not have got up to the scene of action within a week's time. The next best thing that could be done had been done— messengers had been sent off post haste to summon a certain Wesleyan missionary, who of all men had the greatest influence with the Ngatewhatua, and would be patiently heard by the Ngapuhi, although the hapu concerned were professedly converts to Roman Catholicism.

This gentleman resided near the principal Ngatewhatua kainga, and was unluckily absent from home when the news came from the Land Court. Had he been there, the ariki would have probably consulted him, and the war party would consequently not have started. But he was absent on a visit to a distant river.

The reverend gentleman was not very popular among the scattered settlers in the district, and had often made himself obnoxious to them, as they considered. He had lived among the Maori many years; and, being a somewhat narrow-minded man, seemed to look upon the settlers as disturbers of that Christian peace which he believed had covered the tribe among whom he ministered. However, when the emergency arose and he received notice of the impending conflict between the rival tribes, he proved himself equal to the occasion. Taking boat to a suitable point, he there borrowed a horse from a farmer; and, riding at full speed for some thirty miles across the ranges and through the bush, arrived at the township just in the nick of time.

Meanwhile, the rival Maori had been occupied in the usual preliminaries to a fight. The Ngatewhatua had disembarked; and on the following day the two parties were drawn up, facing one another, at a short distance apart. The korero then commenced, and was kept up hour after hour by alternate orators on either side. These delivered themselves in the verbose and florid style customary, running up and down between the lines, and using very unparliamentary language, I have no doubt. The men of the two factions were seated on the ground meanwhile, occasionally grimacing or defying each other.

The modern veneer of civilization and Christianity seemed entirely to have disappeared, and the ancient Maori manners to have superseded it. At length, such a pitch of rage was reached that the war-dance appeared inevitable, and after that nothing would stop the conflict. It was just at this juncture that the missionary rode up. Dismounting, he at once strode between the rival lines, being greeted with growls and opprobrious epithets by the Ngapuhi, and with cries of "Go home! Go home!" from his own flock.

I think I can see that scene now. In the foreground the broad surface of the river, flowing between low banks covered with light scrub. To the right the few houses of the little settlement, with a group of pale-faced Pakeha, men, women, and children, anxiously awaiting the upshot of the "muss." In front, a stretch of open land, partly grassed and partly covered with fern, with stumps and logs here and there visible. Behind it clumps of scrub, and, close to, the line of the heavy bush, extending all round and covering the hill-ranges that rise further back.

In the centre of this scene are the two bands of Maori; brown tatterdemalions in ragged shirts and trousers, armed with guns, and merè, and patu, and axes, some squatting on the ground, some standing erect, all convulsed with anger and ungovernably excited. Before each rank is the ariki, and one or two principal men on either side.

Between the two armies strides the tall, gaunt form of the missionary, his arms raised and gesticulating, his grey hair and beard floating on the wind. Heedless of his reception he begins to talk. He is a perfect master of Maori oratory, with its long quotations from old tradition and from the Bible, its short pithy sentences, its queer interjectional effects. Gradually the tumult quiets down, the Maori begin to listen, the Ngapuhi forget they are Catholics.

For two mortal hours he talks to them, preaches at them. What arguments he uses I cannot say; they are effective ones evidently, for there is a perfect hush among the combatants at last, and all eyes are turned attentively upon the speaker. Finally, he proposes an equal sharing of the sum to be obtained for the disputed land. There is hesitation—he enforces the point, drives it home to the minds of his hearers. Then comes an "Ai!" from the Ngatewhatua ariki, followed by a reluctant "Kuia!" from the Ngapuhi chief. A chorus of "Ai! Ai! Kuia! Kuia!" "Yes! agreed!" resounds on all sides; the dispute is at an end.

But all is not over, the happy moment must be

seized by the minister of the gospel. Standing on a little knoll between the lately hostile taua, he slowly uncovers, raises one hand upwards, looks to heaven, solemnly enunciates the Lord's Prayer. The effect is marvellous, the Maori go down on their knees around him and fervently chorus the words as he utters them, while tears stream from many eyes, and groans of contrition break from many breasts. The prayer finished, the missionary looks about him on the rival warriors, who now crouch like chidden children before him. He commands them, in the Name they have just invoked, to lay aside their weapons, and to be friends. With unquestioning faith and simple alacrity they obey his summons, and Ngapuhi and Ngatewhatua rush into each other's arms.

That night a grand feast is held to cement the new-made friendship; and next day the two chiefs go arm-in-arm to the Land Court, there to conclude the sale of the disputed land, while the bulk of their followers, with much friendly leave-taking, depart on their several ways.

So eventuated the worst difficulty of the kind that has arisen in the North for many years. The affair made no stir beyond the district, for " our special correspondent" was not present, while settlers and officials had very good reasons for not giving publicity to the matter. In view of emigration, and all the rest of it, government, and colonists too, have a disposition to hush up any little perplexities of such a sort; so only a short and garbled account of this narrow escape from a battle reached the Auckland papers, which may be found in them by those who like to look for it.

I think this anecdote may serve to conclude my sketches of Maori manners. It shows the childlike temper of the Maori, their easily excited passions, quick gusts of rage, and equally ready return to docility and good-humour. It is an instance of how modern Maori character is driven by two widely different forces, and of how it oscillates between two systems—the tapu Maori and the tapu Pakeha. It illustrates with strange force—more so than any other incident which has happened in this generation, perhaps—that wonderful power, once so extensive and real, but now almost obsolete except in such rare instances as this—that influence which I have previously spoken of, and have named "the Mana of the Missionary."

CHAPTER VI.

OUR NATURALIST'S NOTE-BOOK.

"IT is impossible to imagine, in the wildest and most picturesque walks of Nature, a sight more sublime and majestic, or which can more forcibly challenge the admiration of the traveller, than a New Zealand forest."—writes an early voyager to this country. From the first, those who visited these shores were struck with the extent and beauty of our forests, the size of the trees, and the wealth of the vegetation. And, at the present day, the emigrant from Scotland or England, brought here into the depths of the bush, fails not to feel his inmost nature responding to the glory and the grandeur of the scenery.

The woodlands of Northern New Zealand may be divided into two general classes, the heavy bush and the light bush. The first is the true primeval forest, the growth, probably, of two or three thousand years. This is by far the most abundant and extensive of the two. There is nothing in Great Britain to afford comparison with it.

The light bush, on the other hand, is not dissimilar to a very wild and luxuriant English wood, if one excepts the difference of the vegetation. It fills up the gullies, and covers the hill-sides, where Maori cultivation once occupied the ground. It is by no means so extensive as the heavy bush, but may be said to fringe it here and there, and to border once populous rivers. These copsewoods spring up very rapidly. Light bush that is only forty years old will rival English woods that have stood a century, in the relative size of the trees. The jungle is so dense that it is often almost impervious to passage altogether, until the axe has cleared a road. It has a rich and fresh appearance when looked at as a whole, a verdancy and wealth of varying tints, a general beauty that seems to make our name for it appear an ill-chosen one ; for we generally call the light bush " scrub."

The heavy bush, in these northern districts, is divisible into two kinds. There is the kauri bush and the mixed bush. The first, as its name implies, is forest where the kauri grows alone, or, at least, preponderates. It has already been described. It is something solemn and tremendous in the last degree, grand and gloomy, and even awful. There are but few trees produced anywhere in the world that can rival the mammoth kauri in bulk. When we consider the closeness with which the trees stand, the uniform mightiness of their endless ranks, stretching on over hill and dale for many a mile, it is not easy to say where we may look to find anything to match or compare with kauri bush.

The mixed bush is very different. Here one is in an actual land of enchantment. Uniformity is gone; unending variety is in place of it. The eye is almost wearied with delight, wonder, and admiration at all around, for there is ever something new, something to prevent the sense of monotony growing up in the mind.

The trees are not of one size, any more than of one kind. Their maximum girth and height fall considerably below that of the largest kauri. Still, one may see kahikatea, kawaka, kotukutuku, matai, miro, pukatea, puriri, rata, rimu, taraire, totara, and many another, whose girth may be as much as thirty feet and more, perhaps; and that may attain a hundred feet or more of height before "heading." Nor are these trees but so many columns. There are trees that branch all round with great domes of foliage. There are some that send several huge limbs upshooting to the sky. There are crooked trees, gnarled trees, bare trees and richly covered ones, leaning trees and fallen trees, a confusion and profusion of arboreal forms.

There is exuberant vegetation above, around, below. Waist-deep in a rich, rare fernery you stand, and, if you have an artistic soul, gaze rapturously about you. From the heights you peer down into the gullies, look abroad over distant sweeps of river, glance through vistas of greenery, over panoramas of wild woodland beauty, carrying your sight away to the far-off hills bathed in sunshine; and all is mantled with the glorious woods.

The mighty trunks and monster limbs of the trees about you are covered with huge masses of moss, shrouded in climbing ivy-ferns, festooned with flowering creepers, and covered with natural hanging gardens to their lofty summits. Around you are the varied forms and colours of more than a hundred different shrubs and trees, evergreen, and flower-bearing in their seasons. There is the cabbage-tree palm, with bare shank and top-knot; the nikau palm, with weird and wondrous frondage; the lancewood, upright and slender, with crest of copper-tinted hair-like leaves; the fern-tree, a vast umbrella of emerald green. There is the twisting squirming rata; the gaunt and powerful kahikatea; the golden kowhai; the dark velvet-covered rimu; the feathery red tawai; the perfumy mangiao; and more that it would take days to particularize. Flowers of bright tint load the trees or shrubs that bear them—scarlet, white, crimson, orange, yellow, blue; and hanging creepers shower festooned cataracts of foliage and blossom down from middle air. And everywhere are ferns, ferns, ferns! abundant, luxuriant, and of endless variety.

You stroll in perfect safety through this gorgeous temple of nature. There is nothing harmful, nothing to fear in all our paradisaic wilderness. No snake, no scorpion, no panther; no danger from beast, or bird, or reptile, or hostile man; nothing to cause the apprehension of the timidest lady. Only a pig, maybe, rushing frantically off in terror at your approach; only a mosquito, sometimes, to remind you you are mortal.

Our Brighter Britain is the natural home of the poet and the artist. Not the least doubt about that. We shall develop great ones some day here. Even the Maori, originally a bloodthirsty and ferocious savage, is deeply imbued with the poetry of the woods. His commonest phraseology shows it. "The month when the pohutukawa flowers;" "the season when the kowhai is in bloom;" so he punctuates time. And the years that are gone he softly names "dead leaves!"

There are over a hundred distinct species of

trees indigenous to this country, and goodness knows how many shrubs and other plants. Sir J. D. Hooker has classified our flora, though doubtless not without omissions. We, the inhabitants of our shanty, are trying to study the natural history of our adopted home. What we have learnt of it —not much, perhaps, yet more than many settlers seem to care to know—we place in our note-book, which I now set forth for all and sundry to criticize.

The Kauri (*Dammara Australis*) is the king of the forest, and must have foremost place. It has already been described fully, in the chapter on our special products, in which I also spoke of kauri-gum, the Kapia of the natives.

The Kahikatea, "white pine" (*Podocarpus dacrydioides*), comes next in order. It attains a hundred and twenty feet or so of stick, and may girth nearly forty feet. It has not much foliage, but rejoices in great, gaunt limbs. Kahikatea bush often occupies marshy ground, and, if unmixed, has a somewhat bare and spectral aspect. The timber is good, but soft, and may be used for deals.

The Totara (*Podocarpus Totara*) attains as great a size. It yields a timber highly prized where kauri cannot be got. The wood is close-grained, and reckoned very valuable. Mottled totara is as much esteemed for cabinet work as mottled kauri.

The Rimu (*Dacrydium cupressinum*) is a beautiful species of cypress; "Black Pine," as bushmen call it. It yields a highly valued timber, used for furniture and interior work. The tree is often as gigantic as the kahikatea, but is stately and finely foliaged.

The Tawai (*Fagus Menziesii*), called "red birch" by settlers, is a favourite for fencing when young. It attains a hundred feet; and yields a good strong timber.

The Tawairaunui (*Fagus fusca*) is a species of the former, known as "black birch." It is stronger and more durable, attains a greater size, but is not so plentiful in the North. The juice is saccharine, like that of the American maple.

The Puriri (*Vitex littoralis*) is sometimes called "teak," or "ironwood." The tree is less than the last. The timber is hard, heavy, very durable, very hard to work, and of a greenish colour. It is commonly used for piles and posts, where the maximum of toughness and durability is required.

The Kowhai (*Sophora tetraptera*) yields timber similar to that of the puriri, but of somewhat inferior quality. It is a fine tree, branching well, and bearing a gold-coloured blossom, whose honey attracts multitudes of tui (parson-birds) in the season.

The Pohutukawa (*Metrosideros tomentosa*) is

called "the Settlers' Christmas Tree," as its scarlet flowers appear about that time. It does not attain more than fifty or sixty feet of height, but is bulky, and has a rich foliage. The wood is most important, being used for knees and ribs in ship building. The bark is astringent, medicinal, and is used in tanneries.

The Hinau (*Elæocarpus dentatus*) produces a good bark for tanning and dyeing. It is not among the largest trees. The Maori used its juice as a dye, and in the process of moku.

The Tanekaha (*Phyllocladus trichomanoides*) is a larger tree again. The timber is used for planks and spars. The bark gives a red-brown dye, formerly used by the Maori, and is exceedingly rich in tannin.

The Kamahi (*Weinmannia racemosa*) is a small tree. It bears a pretty flower, and is a great ornament. The bark is used in tanneries.

The Kohekohe (*Dysoxylum spectabile*) reaches sixty feet. It has magnificent foliage, yields a good timber for fencing, makes first-rate shingles, and contains a bitter principle of tonic quality, like quassia.

The Kawa-kawa (*Piper excelsum*) is a large shrub of the pepper tribe, allied to kava and cubebs. It is ornamental, and has an aromatic scent.

The Pukatea (*Atherosperma N.Z.*) is a tree of

the second largest class. Its timber is soft but durable, and is much used for boat-building. It is a remarkably handsome tree.

The Rata (*Metrosideros robusta*) is of the myrtle tribe. When young it is a creeper and a parasite, called then Ratapiki. It gradually strangles and absorbs the tree round which it climbs, becoming eventually a forest giant, gnarled and twisted. In all its stages it bears a gorgeous scarlet flower. The timber is used for rails, posts, and shingles.

The Ti, or "cabbage-tree palm" (*Cordyline Australis*), grows as high as fifty feet. It branches into various stems, each bearing a head of leaves. The leaf yields a strong fibre. The plentiful seeds are full of oil. The root is farinaceous, and was an item of Maori diet. It is very abundant.

The Toi (*Cordyline indivisa*) is a more ornamental, rarer, and smaller species of "cabbage-tree;" the leaf is larger, handsomer, and also fibre-yielding. Its root is also esculent, like that of the Ti. The name of Toi likewise belongs to a herb (*Barbarea vulgaris*), the leaves of which are eaten like cabbage or spinach.

The Tingahere, or "lancewood" (*Cordyline stricta*), is another species of the same family. It is of very singular appearance, its head resembling a tuft of copper-coloured feathers or hair. There are several more members of this tribe to be seen pretty frequently in the mixed bush.

The Nikau (*Areca sapida*) attains forty or fifty feet. It is a handsome palm, bearing enormous fronds, often fifteen feet or more in length. They are used for thatching wharès in the forest. Within the crown of the leaves is an edible pith, a stick of pinky-white stuff, the size of a man's arm, eating like celery and cocoa-nut in combination; it is refreshing and wholesome.

The Tawhera or Kie-kie (*Freycinetia Banksii*) appears to be sometimes a parasite, sometimes a shrub, and sometimes a small tree. It is a curious plant, with tufts of stringy leaves. It bears a fruit very much esteemed by the Maori, which resembles a green pine-apple, small, and eats like honey and cream.

The Koraka (*Corynocarpus levigata*) was brought to New Zealand by the Maori. It is a small tree, with fine, dark, glossy foliage, which cattle are very fond of. The fruit is edible; the kernel containing "korakine," a narcotic poison. This property, however, appears to be dissipated by heat, as I have known the kernels to be roasted, ground, and made into coffee, without bad result.

The Maire (*Santalum Cunninghamii*) is not a large tree, but the wood is extremely hard, heavy, and finely grained. It was used by the Maori for war-clubs, and is now sawn and utilized for many purposes. Bushmen call it "Black Maire," to distinguish it from the following :—

The Maire-tawhake (*Eugenia Maire*), or "White Maire."

The Maire-aunûi (*Olea Cunninghamii*), which, together with the last, is a much bigger tree than the maire, but does not yield such valuable timber.

The Kotukutuku (*Fuchsia excorticata*) is akin to the fuchsia seen in gardens at home. It is here a huge tree, standing eighty feet in height, and with great girth. The flower is fine, and the fruit agreeable eating.

The Kawaka (*Libocedrus Doniana*) is a grand tree of the largest class. Its timber is dark and heavy, but is too brittle to work well. It serves some purposes, however.

The Mangiao (*Tetranthera calicaris*) is a smaller tree, but one that yields a timber exceptionally useful to carpenters and joiners. It is also largely used in the ship-yards. The wood is fragrant with an aromatic odour, as is also the leaf and blossom.

The Matai, or "Red Pine" (*Podocarpus spicata*), needs special mention. Its wood is durable; soft when fresh, it has the property of hardening with time.

The Miro, "Black Pine" (*Podocarpus ferruginea*), is, like the matai, a large-sized tree. Its timber is close-grained and durable, but is somewhat brittle.

The Ake-ake (*Dodonæa viscosa*) gives a handsome wood for cabinet work, which is said to be imperishable.

The Horopito, or "Pepper-tree" (*Drimys axillaris*) yields also an ornamental timber. Though the tree is of small size its wood is useful for veneers. Its fruit, leaves, and bark contain medicinal properties.

The Ohoeka (*Panax crassifolium*) is a small shrub-like tree, whose wood is noted for singular lightness, flexibility, and elasticity.

The Manuka or Manukau (*Leptospermum scoparium, et ericoides*), is the "ti-tree" of settlers. In one condition it is low shrubbery, not unlike heather, called then Rawiri by the Maori. "Second-growth ti-tree" is like a plantation of cane, coming up very densely. This brushwood is useful for small purposes about a house. It develops into wattles and stakes after twenty years or so; these are of great value for fencing. Finally, the plant becomes one of the largest forest-trees, yielding a hard, close-grained timber. There are red and white varieties. The Maori particularize it as Kahikatoa, when in the tree condition. A sort of manna, which exudes from the plant in all stages, is called by them Piamanuka. Ti-tree springs upon any land that has been cleared or burnt, and comes up densely and rapidly. It is the chief weed the pioneer farmer has to contend with.

The Tawa (*Nesodaphne Tawa*) grows to nearly as great a size as the kahikatea, though branching and spreading more. Its timber, however, is soft and not of value.

The Taraire (*Nesodaphne Taraire*) is a huge and handsome tree of a kindred species. Like the tawa, its wood is light and brittle. The berries of both are eaten, usually after having been boiled.

The Whau (*Entelea arborescens*) is a small tree, noticeable for its fine foliage. The wood is light, and the tree yields a fair substitute for cork.

The Whau-whau-paku (*Panax arborea*) is similarly to be noticed for its elegant glossy leaf.

The Patate (*Schefflera digitata*) is another small tree remarkable on the same account.

The Piripiriwhata (*Carpodetus serratus*) grows to about thirty feet in height. The timber is something like that of the ash, and is excellent for axe-handles, cart-shafts, etc.

The Rama-rama (*Myrtus bullata*) has a good hard wood, but is small. Its pink flower is a great ornament.

The Raukawa (*Panax Edgerleyi*) is a larger ornamental tree.

The Rewa-rewa (*Knightia excelsa*) approaches to the second class of the great trees. It is often a hundred feet in height, but the trunk is slender. Its wood has a splendidly showy grain for cabinet work.

The Tarata (*Pittosporum eugenioides*) is a small tree noted for its purple blossom.

The Tawairauriki (*Fagus Solandri*) is the "White Birch" of settlers. It reaches upwards of a hundred feet; but its timber is inferior and less durable than that of either the red or black varieties.

The Titoki (*Alectryon excelsum*) is one of the larger trees. Its timber is strong, tough, and durable. Its seed is full of a fine fixed oil, which the Maori used to extract and employ as an unguent.

The Manawa, or "mangrove" (*Avicennia officinalis*), is very plentiful in the north, along the shores of tidal waters. The wood is found useful for some minor purposes, and might be used as a source of crude soda, perhaps.

The Ngaio (*Myoporum laetum*) is a small bushy tree, capable of being grown into hedges.

The Neinei (*Dracophyllum latifolium*) is but a small tree. The wood is hard, and is valued for making mallets and the handles of implements.

The Mapau (*Myrsine Urvillei*) affords good material for fencing.

The Mapauriki (*Pittosporum tenuifolium*) has handsome foliage, and a dark purple flower, and can be grown as a shelter tree.

The Kaiwhiria (*Hedycarya dentata*) is remarkable on the same account.

The Houhere (*Populnea Hoheria*) is a fine large tree of the linden kind. Like that tree, its inner bark may be utilized for bass and matting. The flower is snow-white, and very handsome.

The Kaikomako (*Pennantia corymbosa*) will be much cultivated as a garden ornament. The flower is sweet-scented, and the fruit is edible.

This comprises the catalogue of native trees, so far as they are known in our shanty; but, it is said that there are nearly as many more varieties indigenous to the country, though considerably scarcer than any of those mentioned.

There are some shrubs noticeable for one reason and another. We are in the habit of collecting the seeds of such as have remarkably handsome blooms or leafage, and sending them home for our friends to try and raise in their conservatories. A few of our trees and shrubs will bear the English climate, if properly attended to. I have seen fair specimens in botanical gardens. Still, they will never attain their full proportions there. Our favourite flowering or foliage shrubs are these :—

The Akakura (*Metrosideros scandens*), a beautiful climber, which will develop into a tree if allowed to grow. It bears flowers like tufts of crimson silk.

The Akepiro (*Olearia furfuracea*), a shrub with velvety foliage.

The Angi-angi (*Geniostoma ligustrifolium*), a shrub with a white flower.

The Kaikaiatua (*Rhabdothamnus Solandri*). The Maori evidently appreciated some part of this plant, the name of it signifying "Food of Gods," precisely the same title by which the old Greeks spoke of certain dainty mushrooms. It has a fine orange and red-striped blossom.

The Kapuka (*Griselinia littoralis*), a small tree with a yellow-green foliage.

The Karamu or Papaumu (*Coprosma, sp.*), a family of pretty flowering shrubs.

The Karetu (*Hierochloe redolens*), which is not a shrub exactly, but a grass, renowned for its delicious scent.

The Kihi-kihi (*Pittosporum crassifolium*), a shrub with purple flowers, akin to the mapauriki.

The Kohia (*Passiflora tetandra*), the seeds of which yield a bland oil, that may probably be some day utilized.

The Korokio (*Corokia Buddleoides*), a fine erect tree, bearing a conspicuous red berry.

The Koromiko (*Veronica, sp.*); these pretty species are astringent, and their shoots are a remedy for scouring in cattle.

The Kotukutuku (*Fuchsia excorticata*); when full-grown, it becomes one of the largest trees.

The Kowhaingutukaka (*Clianthus puniceus*), bears especially fine red and orange blossoms.

The Kumerahu (*Pomaderris elliptica*), is sweet-scented.

The Mairehau (*Phebalium nudum*) grows well.

The Oho (*Panax Lessonii*), is recommended, but we do not admire it.

The Pere (*Alseuosmia Banksii*), a straggling, spreading bush.

The Pikiarero (*Clematis indivisa*) is very plentiful in the forest. It has fine white, sweet-scented flowers.

The Ratapiki (*Metrosideros Florida*), is a species much the same as the akakura.

The Rohutu (*Myrtus pedunculata*), is pretty.

The Toro (*Persoonia Toro*) becomes a tree. It has rich foliage.

Besides these there are one or two climbers and shrubs that are plentiful everywhere, and must be noticed for other peculiarities. They are these:—

The Kareao (*Rhipogonum scandens*), well-known to settlers under the detested name of "supple-jack." It grows in long, winding canes, the thickness of one's finger, and so horny that they will turn an axe-edge. It often binds acres of trees together in impenetrable thickets, making the bushman's labour excessively difficult. Walking-stick makers export selected canes, and they are split and used as withes. The root is astringent, and is said to resemble sarsaparilla in medicinal virtue.

The Tataramoa (*Rubus Australis*) is equally well-known under the designation of "bush-lawyer." Its stems are flexile, and more like rope than cane, but every part of the plant is fibrous and very strong. It grows in much the same manner as supple-jack, but is luckily not quite so plentiful. It rejoices in abundant foliage, and each leaf is armed with hooked thorns, which lay hold of anything attempting to brush past them. Hence the name; for it is needful to disengage each particular thorn with care and circumspection. There is no pulling away from a bush-lawyer, unless one is prepared to leave clothes and skin hanging on the bush, so tenacious is its hold. The plant belongs to the bramble tribe, and has a white flower and a red berry.

The Mounga-mounga (*Lygodium articulatum*) is the delight of persons camping out. It has a stem like small twine, which depends from the trees in immense bundles of spiral coils. Bunches of it make capital bedding, being, in fact, a natural spring-mattress.

The Tupakihi (*Coriaria ruscifolia*) is a shrub growing chiefly on poor open land. The whole plant is highly astringent, but is also said to contain a narcotic principle. Cattle occasionally eat it, and get poisoned. It bears bunches of juicy berries which are wholesome to eat, but upon them is a seed that is dangerously full of the poisonous principle. The beverage called tutu, which the old Maori esteemed, was made from the berries of this plant. When it was boiled with a certain seaweed (*Porphyra*) a nutritious jelly was formed. Tutu was probably not universally known among the Maori, but only to certain tribes. It appears to have been intoxicating, for warriors who required a "drop of somethink short" were accustomed to imbibe it on the eve of battle.

New Zealand is well-known to be a great place for ferns. They exist in incredible profusion everywhere. Botanists have enumerated a hundred and thirty indigenous species, of which some forty are peculiar to the country. We are always sending roots, seeds, and dried species home, but I cannot attempt to catalogue them. Several kinds resembling that beautifully delicate fern called the maidenhair are among our commonest species. Their luxuriance is astonishing. They cover acres and acres of ground in the bush, and come up to one's waist and armpits.

The Tuakura (*Dicksonia squarrosa*) and the Ponga (*Cyathea dealbata*) are the two principal varieties of fern-tree. Groves of them, overshadowing some lonely creek, at the bottom of a wild, wooded gully, are indeed a sight to see. Growing to twenty, thirty, or forty feet in height, the graceful drooping fronds that spread around a single tree form a natural arbour, capable of sheltering a number of persons.

The Raurau (*Pteris aquilina*, var. *esculenta*) is a fern of the nature of English bracken. It covers all the better-class open lands, and occurs among the undergrowth of the bush. It sometimes grows very large, the fronds overtopping one's head as one walks or rides through it. The root is a Maori edible.

The ivy-ferns, climbing-ferns, or creeper-ferns (*Polypodia, sp., Hymenophylla sp.*), are very beautiful. They are everywhere in the bush, ascending to the tops of the tallest trees, twining on every limb, and throwing out bunches of fronds to hide it. Some have broad, glossy leaves as big as a table-top; others are digitate, pedatisect, tripinnate, and all the rest of it, or assume strange new shapes, like that of the kidney-fern (*Trichomanes reniforme*), for instance.

Like the ferns, the mosses of the country are legion in number, and marvellously luxuriant in growth. They, too, are everywhere. Great masses of moss form hanging-gardens on the trees; for, collecting a quantity of detritus and moisture, a sort of soil is formed, in which small ferns, tawhera, orchids, plants of various kinds, and fungi, flourish. In and about these hanging-gardens, these ferneries high up upon the great trees, are the homes and habitations of birds, rats, bees, beetles, lizards, and butterflies.

The Harakeke or Korati (*Phormium tenax*) is the justly celebrated New Zealand flax. It is plentiful everywhere, on bush-land and open-land, rich soil and poor soil, hill and dale, from the Reinga to the Bluff. Throughout the North you cannot go a hundred yards in any direction without seeing a clump of it. In many districts of both islands it covers hundreds of acres entirely.

Flax resembles the English flag, or iris, in appearance, but the blades are thicker, heavier, and glossy. Usually, from four to six feet long, in favourable situations they grow to ten or twelve feet. The colour is a bright green, variegated in some of the species with white, yellow, or red. The plant grows in dense clumps, or bushes, and from the centre of each root rises a tall stem bearing flowers, white, yellow, salmon, flesh-pink, red, in different varieties. The flowers are peculiarly rich in honey; and Maori children are fond of sucking them. The resulting seed is oily and resinous, the seed-stems being commonly used for torches.

The leaves of the harakeke are composed of a strong fibre, which ranks next to silk in degree of tenacity. The whole plant is impregnated with gum, quantities of which are found about the base of the leaves. The gum is astringent, and the root is rich in tannin. This fresh gum was used by the Maori for every purpose of cement and glue. The root had its place in their pharmacopeia.

From the earliest times that Europeans had any knowledge of New Zealand, this flax-fibre has excited great attention. The quality of the Maori manufactures from it was sufficient to arouse earnest inquiry into the nature of the material. The robes and dresses they wove out of phormium yarn were articles often of considerable beauty, finish, and design. The kaitaka, for instance, made from a choice variety of flax, has a gloss like silk or satin, and, though thick, is perfectly soft and flexible. All these garments were so durable that they could be handed down from generation to generation.

But the labour involved in making these articles was prodigious, and would have rendered them above all price in a community where an individual's time was commutable into cash. The fibre was separated by hand, and freed from the all-permeating gum by toilsome manipulative processes. This work of freeing the fibre from gum has always been the great difficulty. Even yet success has not been wholly achieved. No European machinery or process has yet been perfected that will turn out an article like the Maori manufacture, and at a practicable cost. If it could be done, the fabric would bring immense wealth to this country.

Very early in this century phormium fibre was brought to Sydney and to England. The manufacture of cloth from it was essayed at Knaresborough, in Yorkshire, but it was found that the fibre was destroyed by boiling it with chemicals, which had been resorted to for removal of the gum. However, it soon became known as of value for cordage, canvas, and paper-making. Phormium rope, tested against the best Manilla rope, bulk for bulk, has been over and over again proved the stronger and most durable.

Many mills have been erected, and much capital

sunk in the production of the dressed fibre, and in experimenting to render it more workable at commensurate cost. In the North less has been done in this way than elsewhere. There are mills at Whangarei, at Aratapu, and at sundry other places; but it is evident that further south must lie the chief fields of flax industry. In Taranaki and in Westland, for example, there are miles and miles of nothing but flax. The supply of leaf is there simply inexhaustible.

In the commercial world New Zealand flax-fibre was highly esteemed at one time, but has fallen out of favour. During 1873 the colony exported dressed fibre to the value of £143,799, but in 1875 this export fell to £11,742, and, though it has recovered slightly, it has not reached the original standard. This has been owing to the action of English rope-makers, who continue to prefer Manilla hemp, and to depreciate the price of our product, in spite of its acknowledged superiority. A short-sighted policy on their part, it promises to result well for the colony. Unable to find a market for the raw material, New Zealanders are beginning to manufacture rope, canvas, and paper themselves. There is not a doubt that their products will take the foremost place, and bring great wealth to the country.

Experimenting with flax has been a regular

craze. Many a man has lost all his capital in it. You have only to see what the Maori have done with the fibre, and to recognize the enormous supply of the material, to get bitten by this mania. It seems so manifestly certain that there must be a way of working up the material by machinery at a reasonable cost, and producing a fabric such as the Maori did, which could be sold at a profit. Only find out the way to do it, and the fortunes that could be made would be boundless in extent.

In the green state, the flax leaf is most useful to both settler and Maori. Every purpose for which cordage of any kind is wanted, is easily supplied by cutting some leaves from the nearest clump, splitting and tying them together. They look unsightly, but they are just as strong as need be. Whether it is a bridle, a halter, a boat-cable, or a boot-lace that is required, green flax-leaf out of the nearest bush supplies it. And the Maori plait kits and baskets for all purposes with it.

Take it altogether, in the green state and in the manufactured condition, in the present and prospectively, as what it has been and what it will become, there is nothing in the country to equal the value of the phormium. Few countries have a natural product so useful, and of such vast importance to their future welfare.

The vegetable edibles of the bush have already been alluded to in the description of Maori manners. There would be no need for any one to starve, if he were lost in the forest for months, did he but know the native esculents, even if he were unable to supplement them by catching birds or fish. Almost every Maori—at any rate of the old school —is a good practical botanist and naturalist. He knows the properties and native name of every plant; and he knows the habits of each bird, or fish, or insect, and how to catch it. When the Pakeha condescends to go to the Maori for instruction in these particulars, he will be sure to gain something by it.

The principal edible, because the most widespread, was the fern-root. It was prepared in several ways. The most elaborate consisted in macerating, steaming, and kneading the gummy fibrous stuff, and keeping the resulting mess until a kind of fermentation began in it. The readiest way was to simply roast the scraped root, then to beat it into softness between two stones. When cold, this last became hard like biscuit. It is tolerably nutritious, but not particularly nice, according to Pakeha notions.

The root of the ti, and of the toi, too, I believe, is far better food, but was neither so plentiful nor so easily grubbed up. Baked or boiled it is not bad eating, being very farinaceous. The earliest missionary settlers made beer from a wort of it. Whether this was known to the Maori previous to the advent of the Pakeha, I have been unable to discover.

The pith of the nikau is wholesome, nutritious, and palatable. The tree is plentiful enough in the North. Unlike the root of the cabbage-tree just mentioned, it is eaten raw. There is a bushy grass (*Gahnia* and *Cladium*), strong spiny stuff, in the forest, which also has an edible pith.

The root of the raupo (*Typha angustifolia*), the swamp-grass of which the Maori construct their wharè, is edible, similarly to that of the cabbage-tree. Punga-punga, the pollen of the raupo, used to be made into bread.

There are one or two other roots and piths also esculent, but neither so good nor so plentiful as those just recorded. There are the fruits of the hinau, rimu, matai, miro, kahikatea, koraka, tawa, kohekohe, taraire, tawhera, and other trees and shrubs. And there is the interior of the stem of one of the fern trees.

There are the native spinach or Renga-renga (*Tetragonia expansa*), the Pana-pana, or cress (*Cardamine hirsuta*), and the Reti-reti, or sorrel (*Oxalis magellanica*), which do for salad and green vegetables. As they are plentiful, they might be more freely used by settlers and bushmen than they are.

To them may be added the Toi (*Barbarea vulgaris*), a herb which served the ancient Maori as cabbage. Then there is a native celery (*Apium australe*), a nettle (*Urtica incisa*), and a dandelion (*Taraxacum dens-leonis*), all of which might be eaten. The Maori also made use of the root of an orchid (*Gastrodia Cunninghamii*), and the root of a bindweed (*Convolvulus sepium*). They called the first Hirituriti, and the latter Panake. These roots are farinaceous and nourishing, and were baked and consumed in large quantities.

The three plants cultivated by the Maori— Kumera (*Ipomœa Batatas*), Hue (*Cucurbita, sp.*), and Taro (*Caladium esculentum*), are all to be found growing wild. There are also now to be found wild many of our garden vegetables, including the potato, tomato, capsicum, tobacco, cabbage, cape gooseberry (*Physalis Peruviana*), watercress—called Kowhiti by the natives—and many more.

Lastly, the Maori made use of several seaweeds and a number of fungi. But, as Britons at home persist in despising all other fungi but the field mushroom and the truffle, I suppose they will hardly take to such food here, dainty though it is. One fungus (*Hirneola, sp.*) is gathered here to a small extent for export to China. It fetches about 15*s*. to £1 per cwt., and about £1000 worth are annually exported. It grows plentifully on certain trees. The field mushroom (*Agaricus campestris*), well known in England, has appeared on our paddocks, sometimes in enormous quantities. Together with its congener the horse-mushroom (*A. arvensis*), this fungus is not indigenous, according to Maori information on the subject. I have heard the species called "Harori-kai-pakeha," which conveys the idea that the field mushroom is an introduced species. But the Maori applied the name of Harori to several species belonging to the families *Agaricus, Amanita, Lepiota*, etc., which we call "toadstools." They were accustomed to eat certain of these, and do so still, if they happen to find them in the bush. All fungi growing on trees they call Hakeke, or Popoiahakeke. Of these, they were accustomed to eat the three or four species of *Hirneola*, which are indigenous, and one or two *Polypori* besides. One of the latter tribe yielded them a surgical appliance. A mushroom they name Putawa, is a *Boletus*. Probably more than one species of this family was customarily eaten. The Maori also ate the Pukurau (*Lycoperdon Fontainesii*), and possibly other species of puff-balls besides. They knew the esculent value of the

Pekepekekiore (*Hydnum Clathroides*), but their chiefest dainty and most esteemed treasure among fungi, is the Paruwhatitiri, or "thunder-dirt" (*Ileodictyon cibarium*). The volva of this extraordinary fungus is eaten, and is regarded as a great dainty. There are many species of fleshy fungi in the bush, but little is known of them, either by Maori, settlers, or scientists.

New Zealand did without quadrupeds in the old times, save and except the kio e, or rat. This was a delicacy much esteemed by Maori bon-vivants, and was regularly hunted by them with great ceremonial. It is rapidly becoming extinct, only being found now in the remote recesses of the forest. The Norwegian rat, which centuries ago exterminated the aboriginal British rat, has somehow come over here with the Pakeha, and is rapidly rendering the kiore a thing of the past, while spreading through the land in its place.

There was some talk of the discovery of a kind of otter, but, I believe, that has been proved a myth altogether. There were some bats, and there was the dog, kararehe or peropero. The kararehe, however, was never wild to any extent. It had been brought here by the Maori, and was kept domesticated by them. They prized its flesh for food, and its skin for robes.

Captain Cook's pigs are now numerous everywhere, as has been described in another chapter. Besides them, cattle, goats, sheep, and cats are now found wild in certain localities, and in considerable number.

We have, luckily, no snakes, and the only reptiles are pretty little ngarara, or lizards (*Mocoa zelandica*, and *M. ornata*), together with a few frogs in some districts. The Maori have legends respecting enormous ngarara that they say once existed here. They have a tale of these taniwha which is somewhat parallel to our nursery stories of dragons.

Instead of animals New Zealand possessed an extraordinary class of gigantic birds, the famous moa, in fact. The kiwi (*Apteryx*) remains as an example of this family. The kiwi, of which there are four known species, varies from the size of a common hen to that of a goose. It has neither wings nor tail; and its dull brown feathers resemble coarse hair. It has a long flexible bill, and thick powerful legs, which divide into four strong claws.

The kiwi is a night-bird, lying hid by day. It is very shy, disappearing from the neighbourhood of settlements and haunting the recesses of the forest, where I have found it to be still very plentiful. The kiwi lays a very large egg in proportion to its size. A bird of four and a half pounds will lay an egg of fourteen ounces weight. The Maori used to catch considerable numbers of them, and do still in some parts, using their flesh for food, their skins for leather, and their feathers for weaving into chiefs' robes. Having eaten kiwi old and young, baked and boiled, roast and fried, I am able to state that its meat is tougher and more tasteless than barbecued boot-soles.

The Maori have two ways of catching kiwi. They hunt them with dogs trained to the work; that is one method. The dog flushes the kiwi, which runs swiftly and silently off among the undergrowth. The dog follows by scent. At last the kiwi is driven into some swamp, where it half buries itself in the mud, and stupidly stands till it is caught.

Another plan is to light a fire by night in some secluded and likely thicket, the hunter lying concealed near. He imitates the cry of the kiwi, and so lures it to the fire, where it stands dazzled and stupefied till he seizes it. A party I was out with once caught a dozen birds so one night.

The now extinct moa appear to have been very similar to kiwi, only of gigantic size. Plenty of their skeletons are found, enabling naturalists to tell us all about them, corroborated by the tradition of the Maori. They seem to have been in existence up to the end of last century, and, till lately, it was thought that individual specimens might even yet be found in unexplored localities. This hope no longer remains.

There were three families of moa (*Dinornis, Aptornis, Palapteryx*), subdivided into several species. The smallest was five feet, and the largest sixteen feet in height. They were of enormous bulk, too; one species had legs thicker than a man's thigh. But huge as they were, they were shy and stupid, and not formidable, so that the Maori were able to run them down and club them to death.

If the moa's egg was as large in proportion to the bird as the kiwi's is to it, it must have been a monster. And if, as naturalists lead us to infer, the moa was but a magnified kiwi in all respects, it is to be supposed that its flesh would be correspondingly tougher and coarser. In that case, I do not see why the Maori should be blamed for turning cannibal in preference to eating it.

The first voyagers to New Zealand speak with special unction of the multitudes of birds, and especially of singing birds. They could scarcely do so now. The native birds have noticeably diminished in number, though they are yet to be found plentifully enough in the remote bush. The Maori say in their picturesque manner—

"When the big Pakeha bird (ship) swam upon the sea to Ahinamaui, the little Maori birds flew away."

Some have thought that the introduction of honey-bees has caused the disappearance of honey-sucking birds. A more probable reason is that advanced by Dr. Buller, namely, that the Norwegian rat is the real cause. This little beast swarms throughout the forest country, and robs nests of eggs and young.

But the Maori birds are by no means so few in number as some writers would have us believe; and they are being rapidly augmented by numerous species from other countries, imported and acclimatized, which are thriving apace and multiplying prodigiously. I shall only have room to mention a few of our native species, such as are peculiarly noticeable or comparatively common.

The Tui (*Prosthemadera N.Z.*) is commonly known as "parson-bird," from two white projecting feathers on the neck, which exactly parody a clergyman's falling bands. It is somewhat larger than the English starling, with plumage resembling it, but more metallic in colour and glossier. It sucks honey from flowers, and eats berries. It has a cheerful song, and can imitate like a mocking-bird. I have often seen scores of tui at a time on blossoming kowhai trees. Tui give regular concerts in the early morning, and the motions of the bird when singing resemble those of a preacher, a curious addition to the likeness conveyed by its "bands." Tui fatten so excessively on phormium seeds, that the Maori have a fable that they peck a hole in their breasts, to let the superfluous oil out. The bird is a favourite for caging, both with Maori and settlers. It can be taught to whistle tunes and articulate words. It is good eating.

The Kuku (*Carpophaga N.Z.*) is a wood-pigeon, a good deal larger than the English species. It has splendid plumage, of a dark, flashing, metallic green, with touches of red, and a white breast. It appears to be migratory, coming down in flocks every now and then, especially when the cabbage trees are in seed. On these oily beans it gets absurdly fat, like the tui, so much so, that when you shoot a bird and it falls to the ground, you find the skin split, and the fat oozing forth. The kuku appear in hundreds and thousands sometimes, and numbers may easily be shot. The Maori snare them and spear them by scores. They are capital eating.

The Weka (*Ocydromus Earli*) is found plentifully in the woods. Settlers call it the "bush-hen." It has a pretty mottled plumage of partridge tints, and its flesh eats like grouse. The weka is somewhat larger than the English water-hen. It is getting less abundant every year. There is a larger bird in the bush of kindred species, rarer, and distinguished by more showy colours, which I have seen once or twice, but could not identify. Probably it may have been a cross between the weka and the common domestic fowl.

The Pukeko (*Porphyrio melanotus*) is a splendid water-bird, larger than the biggest duck. It is known as the "swamp-hen." Its purple colouring and crimson beak give it quite a royal and magnificent appearance. This bird is getting rapidly more numerous instead of the contrary. It has quite taken to Pakeha domination, apparently, and could probably be domesticated. The pukeko was brought here by the Maori. It is fine eating.

The Kaka (*Nestor meridionalis*) is a large bird of the parrot kind. Its plumage is of a greenish brown, with scarlet under the wings. It is common and good eating. There are several varieties of kaka, some in which the colouring is dull, and others in which it is richly variegated. It eats insects and berries, and sucks the honey from flowers. Its note is harsh and clamorous.

The Kakariki (*Platycercus N.Z.*) comprehend several species of small parrot or parrakeet. They are distinguished by brilliant emerald-green and scarlet feathers. Occasionally a good many may be seen. They are noisy fellows—like all parrots.

The Kuimako or Kohorimako (*Anthornis melanura*) is a bird about the size of a thrush. Its plumage is olive-green, with purple about the head. It has a sweet note, that has been compared to the tinkling and chiming of silver bells; hence its common name, "the bell-bird." It is our nightingale. Once chorusing in flocks, singing at daybreak, it may still be often heard, but, sad to say, is getting scarcer.

The Kahu (*Circus Gouldi*) is chief among several of the hawk tribe. It looks almost eagle-like, as its broad wings skim across the sky. It is a sad marauder among the settler's poultry. Sometimes two or three of them will combine and attack a turkey or lamb. They do good by keeping down rats on open ground.

The Ruru (*Spiloglaux N.Z.*) is a small brown owl, heard everywhere at night. It is called the "morepork," from its doleful iteration of apparently that word. There is also a singular green owl-parrot, the kakapo (*Stringops habroptilus*), which lives in holes in the ground. It attacks sheep and tears their backs. It does not belong to our catalogue, as it is not found in the Land of the Kauri, principally inhabiting Canterbury and Otago.

I believe there are one or two other species of owls besides them.

The Kaiaia (*Hieracidea Brunnea*) is a sparrow-hawk, smaller than the kahu. It will probably have its work cut out in keeping down the English sparrows that have been introduced, and are likely to get too numerous. By the same native name the "quail-hawk" (*Hieracidea N.Z.*) is also known. Both of these hawks are so exceedingly fierce that they will attack anything, either singly or in concert. They have even been known to fly at men, and to pounce at game in their hands.

The Patatai (*Rallus Philippensis*) is a small land-rail, plumaged much like a partridge. It may not infrequently be seen; and makes a dainty dish.

The Matuku (*Botaurus pœciloptilus*) is a bittern, long-legged and billed. It is of dull hues, and its monotonous boom may be heard from the swamps. The Maori are expert at catching them; but I cannot say that bittern-meat is good. There is a smaller species of bittern, a blue heron, and possibly others of the family, all known under the common name of matuku.

The Kotare (*Halcyon vagans*) is a kingfisher, whose bright plumage flits continually through the mangroves, where it principally makes its home. It is larger than our English species, and of much the same hues, sea-green and ultramarine, with orange-tawny under the wings.

The Kawau (*Phalacrocorax, sp.*) is one of the commonest birds. There are half a dozen distinct species, known to us by the general name of shag or cormorant. They have a black back and a white breast. Some have blue, green, and other tints of colouring. They build in trees, in large "shaggeries," and haunt the seashore and the banks of the rivers.

The Kuaka (*Limosa Baueri*) is the bird spoken of as "curlew" and "grey snipe" by colonists. Large flocks are to be seen on our rivers, feeding on the mud-banks. When they are assembled in numbers, it is often possible to creep cautiously within range, and take a pot-shot at the crowd as it rises. A number may thus be bagged. The Maori used to net them by night. They are fairly good eating.

The Titi or "mutton-bird" (*Puffinus brevicaudus*) is a species of petrel common throughout the South Sea. They breed in burrows far inland, consorting in immense flocks. An island in Bass' Straits is resorted to by them annually, in such incredible numbers, that one estimate, arrived at by calculating the cubic space they occupied, gave a hundred and fifty millions as their probable numbers. On our coasts they often come in legions. The Maori catch them by stretching nets along the seashore at night. The birds, flying low, and returning after dark to their inland roosting-places, are thus trapped in great quantities. The Maori used to preserve them in calabashes, partly cooked, and potted in the oily fat that had exuded from them. They were thus made into a sort of " canned provisions," which might be stored up against times of dearth, or made an article of trade with inland tribes.

The Koreke (*Coturnix N.Z.*), the native quail, was once very plentiful, though more so on the grassy downs of the south than here. The natives used to net koreke in great quantities, much as they did the titi and kuaka. Now, the bird is scarce in our part of the country. Only rarely do we see a flock of half a dozen or so. But their place is amply filled by various imported species of game-birds, now getting very plentiful.

The Huia (*Heteralocha Gouldi*) must just be mentioned, as it is one of the most striking of New Zealand species. It is only found in the mountains of Wellington and Nelson provinces, consequently not in our districts. The huia is a large bird, of a uniform glossy black colour, shot with green. It has a long bent bill, and brilliant orange wattles.

The Koheperoa (*Eudynamis Taitensis*) is a long-tailed, brown-plumaged cuckoo, which comes here from the South Sea Islands in the month of October —our May. Its habits appear to be much the same as those of the English cuckoo. I only once saw one closely, but have heard them oftener.

The Popo or Popotea (*Orthonyx albicilla*) is a little brown bird with a white head, which sings like a chaffinch, and principally lives about rata trees. We see them not infrequently.

The Riroriro (*Gerygone flaviventris*) is a little warbler seen about in company with the tauhau.

The Toutou (*Miro longipes*) is a small grey and white bird, which some people have said is called the New Zealand robin. It is to be seen in the bush now and then, and seems tame, but *we* prefer to call another species *our* robin.

The Pihoi (*Anthus N.Z.*) is the so-called native "lark." It is a ground pipit, and may often be seen fluttering and chirping about a bush road.

The Korohea (*Turnagra Hectori*) is the native thrush, and a poor imitation it is of the English throstle. It is scarce. Sometimes its song may be listened to with pleasure.

The Kokako (*Glaucopis Wilsoni*) is a crow, and is not uncommon in the Kaipara. It has blue wattles on the beak. Its note is peculiar, being sometimes a low, hollow boom, and at others a shrill and somewhat bell-like tone.

The Putoto (*Ortygometra Tabuensis*) is a crake, often confounded by settlers with the patatai. It is a smaller bird altogether, having partridge tints on the back, and a grey breast. It chiefly inhabits raupo swamps.

The Torea, or oyster-catcher (*Haematopus longirostris*) is one of the sea-coast birds, and is often to be seen about our tidal rivers. It is a black bird.

The Kotuku, or crane (*Ardea syrmatophora*), must just be mentioned, though none of us ever saw one. But the Maori have a proverb—"as rare as the kotuku."

There are various species of duck indigenous to the country, and seen in great flocks on the rivers. Some of them have really fine plumage, and others are dull in colour. We shoot and eat them all indiscriminately, and consider them very good. The species we have identified in the Kaipara and Hokianga are—the Putangi, or "paradise-duck" (*Casarca variegata*); the grey duck, or Parera (*Anas superciliosa*); the brown duck, an allied species or variety of the last; the Papanga, or "teal," or "widgeon" (*Fuligula N.Z.*), and some other varieties that may be imported birds, or crosses, or other native species. Besides these are numerous species of seabirds: gulls, albatross, tern, skua, penguin, etc.

We never eat them, of course, though the Maori do, as they occasionally shoot some for the sake of their feathers.

The Tauhau (*Zosterops lateralis*) is a beautiful little green bird, much like a wren. It has a gold or silvery ring round the eye. It is much seen about gardens and clearings, and settlers know it as the "blight-bird." It frequents second-growth ti-tree, where its little mossy nest and four or five pale blue eggs may often be found. This bird is said to have only recently come to the country, from no one knows where. It is quite at home now, and we see its nest oftener than that of any other species.

The Waka-waka (*Rhipidura flabellifera*) is *the* robin of our Brighter Britain. It is a fantail, or flycatcher. It has dark brown tints pied with white and black. When one is working or travelling in the bush, a pair of these dear little birds will stay with one all day. They appear beside you in the morning, and remain with you till night. They flutter and flirt about you, sitting on twigs and regarding you with a bright beady eye, whilst chirruping in a soft, unobtrusive undertone. We find their nests sometimes, in bush-lawyer or supple-jack clumps, or in birch-trees. They are curiously built with spiders' webs.

Many a rough, rude bushman has grown quite sentimental regarding these little companions of man, and would visit with dire vengeance any attempt to harm them. The Maori, as usual, have quaint superstitious fancies about them. An old fellow, who in youth had been "out" with Hone Heke, was once my companion on a journey through the forest. He alluded feelingly to the waka-waka that, as usual, were fluttering about us.

"Ah!" he said, "they are little spirits" (atua nuke-nuke). "They come to see what men are doing in the bush by day, and go back to tell God at night. To-night they will say, 'we saw the Maori and the Pakeha together in the forest. They ate of the same, and drank of the same, and slept together in one blanket, and were brothers.' And God will say, 'It is good!'"

These are the birds known to the naturalists of our shanty, but there are plenty more species, rarer, or whose habitat is limited to districts south of this. And now, too, any ornithological catalogue of the country must contain the names of numerous acclimatised species, many of which are getting almost too abundant. We have many English song-birds and insect-eaters; larks and linnets and thrushes, etc. And we have game in any quantity in some districts, rapidly extending all over the islands, of the following descriptions : The English pheasant (*Phasianus colchicus*), the Chinese pheasant (*Phasianus torquatus*), the partridge (*Perdix cinerea*), the Californian quail (*Ortyx Californicus*), the Australian quail (*Coturnix pectoralis*), and some others.

I have already said something about insects, when describing our home life. I spoke of the mosquito (*Culex*), of the sandfly (*Simulium*), and of the kauri-bug (*Polyzosteria N.Z.*). I think I also mentioned a certain not wholly unknown and *nimble* creature, which the Maori are accustomed to term Pakeha-nuke-nuke, or "little stranger."

Then there is the Cricket (*Cicada*), which swarms on the clearings, eating down the grass, and doing damage in the gardens and fields. It is the chief enemy of farmers. We have to keep large flocks of turkeys on the clearings to keep down the crickets. They devour the insect greedily, getting to a marvellous size on the food, and acquiring a delicacy and flavour far beyond that of stubble-fed birds. A plague of caterpillars also appears sometimes, which must be combated by similar means.

We have flies in hosts, innumerable spiders, some of them as big as walnuts, with hairy legs like a crab's claws, huge flying locust-grasshoppers, goat-chafers, cock-chafers, dragon-flies, beetles, and butterflies, the last not often remarkable for size or brilliance. There are two unique creatures that must have special reference made to them.

The Hotete is the so-called "vegetating caterpillar." It is a grub two or three inches long, and out of its head there grows a parasitic fungus (*Sphaeria Robertsii*), in the form of a long spire or blade, six or seven inches in length, with a seed-spur on the top. The natives eat the hotete. It is the larva of *Hepialus virescens*, a kind of locust.

The Weta (*Deinacrida heteracantha*) is a creature of the locust form living in dead-wood. Its body may reach to three inches in length, and be about the thickness of one's thumb. It is covered with horny scales, resembling those of a shrimp, but of a darker brown colour. The head is perfectly black, and resembles a small lobster, with the claws and mandibles projecting downwards. There are two large staring eyes, and two immense antennæ. It has six legs, the latter pair being very strong and large, while all are armed with serrated edges or files, and with hooked claws. Behind, there is a horny, wedge-like spine. From the hinder claws to the tip of the antennæ the weta may measure sixteen inches, if a full-grown specimen. It bores its way through dead-wood, in which it lives. Sometimes you get a weta on your clothes, and feel horrified; but it is perfectly harmless, though you will have to take it in pieces to get it off you. The larva of this reptile, a huge sickly-white maggot, is a great prize to a Maori. He fixes it on a stick, toasts it at the fire, and eats it with every sign and expression of extravagant delight. I must say that the odour of the toasted grub is very appetizing, still, I never could bring myself to try one.

The poisonous spider of Taranaki—if, indeed, it really exists—is unknown in our part of the country. We have numbers of bees. Nearly every hollow tree contains comb. The shanty is seldom without a bucketful of honey, for the consumption of those who like it. These bees are a naturalized importation though; there were none indigenous, I understand.

When touching on the Maori commissariat I alluded to our fish. We have, indeed, a wealth of fish in all the tidal waters. Sharks, schnapper, rock-cod, mackerel, mullet, herring, sole, halibut, albacore, barracouta, king-fish, and others. All sorts of ways of fishing may be practised successfully. One can always get fresh fish for supper, for half an hour's trouble; and a day or night's netting or spearing will provide ample store for smoking, drying, or salting. There are eight kinds of whales, so bay-whaling is carried on round the coast. There are also seals and dolphins.

The Maori think most of shark-meat, which

they cure largely. It is stinking stuff. We are always ready to lend a hand at a shark-hunt, which is good sport, but we decline our share of the plunder. We prefer the substantial schnapper, the goodly whapuka or kanae, or the luscious porahi.

Cockles, mussels, clams, mutton-fish, oysters, and other molluscs abound in the mud and on the rocks. In the freshwater streams are eels, lampreys, and whitebait; and now salmon and trout have been introduced into many of them, and are doing well. People who admire a fish diet should come here. They could revel in profusion of it, as the Maori did and do.

When the naturalist's note-book of our shanty shall have become enlarged and more copious, I may possibly be able to add to this slight sketch of the natural history of Northern New Zealand. But perhaps I have already said more than enough to weary the hapless reader.

CHAPTER VII.

THE DEMON DOG—A YARN.

OLD COLONIAL is good at spinning yarns, and there is one of his I should like to put in here, because it is so thoroughly descriptive of the very first essays at pioneer-farming in this district.

One night, when we were all comfortably settled to our pipes round the fire in our shanty, by general request, Old Colonial began as follows—

"Ah! it's a good many years since I first came up into this district, new as it is even yet. Near as Auckland is, comparatively, the people there know no more about us than the folks at home. I've stuck close to the district, as I like it, and think it's as good as any in the colony. But, you see, other people don't. New-chums, if they hear of the Kaipara at all, learn that it's very hilly, and all bush of one kind or another, and that frightens them; so they go south to the open districts. And then, Government is more interested in getting settlers elsewhere than here. People are told that there are no roads up here, and that the Maori hold the greater part of the land. That is enough for them, of course, and they don't come up to see for themselves. As there is no decent map of the colony available as yet, naturally they cannot know that what with our tidal rivers and freshwater creeks, intersecting the district in all directions as they do, we really want no roads, as no one will settle in the back country until the water frontage is filled up, which will not be for many years yet. Then, our Maoris are the best neighbours any one could wish to live among, and are only too well pleased to sell lands and welcome new settlers.

"After all, we are just a trifle out of the way, you must allow. Although we've got Tom's little steamer now, running regularly on the rivers, still, communication with the city means two transhipments and a portage, with tremendously heavy freights, unless you can charter a cutter yourself and go all round by the open sea. So that, though we settlers may think the Kaipara in every way desirable, there's good reason for those who have never been in it to give their preference to the Waikato, or Wanganui, or Canterbury.

"However, I dare say you are beginning to wonder what all this has to do with my tale of old times.

Not being a professional story-teller, I suppose I'm not over good at shaping a yarn, especially at the beginning, but—there's some more rum in that bottle!—if you'll have patience I shall get into the thick of it directly.

"Well, the district being what it is in this year of grace eighteen hundred and seventy, you may easily suppose that, sixteen years ago, it was quite like coming into an undiscovered world to come up here. At that time I believe that Karl was really the only settler in the entire tract of country; and as that comprises between two and three thousand square miles, and as there were no more Maoris then than there are now, probably not more than a total of a thousand altogether in all the little kainga round, it could scarcely be called a populous part of New Zealand.

"I don't know what had tempted Karl to select up this way. Probably accident led him into the Kaipara, and when here he saw his way to something. There is no doubt that if things had gone straight he might now have been one of the richest men in the province. However, things did not go straight, and why they didn't is the subject of my tale.

"I first happened upon Karl in Auckland, sixteen years ago it is now, as I have just told you. He was a German by race, but English by education, and seemed to have knocked about the world a good bit. He was a tall, powerful man, quiet and composed in general demeanour, rather pleasant to get on with, well-informed and gentlemanly, but with a decidedly rough and wild side to his character, which only appeared now and then. I agreed to hire with him for a spell, and accompanied him on his return to this district.

"A year or so previously Karl had purchased Hapuakohe on the Arapaoa river—that is the place we went to help with the cattle at the other day, and the best farm in the district it is now. Karl had got about six thousand acres dirt cheap, as land goes to-day, and had settled on it at once. Being the first purchaser from the tribe, the Maoris of the district held him in high esteem, and a lot of the young men gave him their labour at the start, as part of the bargain. They helped him to get timber and build a shanty and sheds, to enclose a bit of ground for potatoes, and so on, and to put up a stockyard. Then Karl chartered a small vessel from the Manukau, and brought up his various necessaries—a few head of cattle, some pigs, fowls, a dog or two, and so forth.

"Of course he was going to commence with running cattle in the bush, as we do at present, but a happy chance saved him from the necessity of this, and all its attendant hard work. Some part of his place had been in Maori occupation comparatively recently, and was only covered with fern and ti-tree bush. The season was a very dry one, unusually so, and Karl was able to burn off all this stuff tolerably clean. He still had some capital left, and with that was able to buy grass seed, though at a ruinous price in those times, and sow down his burns. By this means he got something like a thousand acres of pasture after the rains came—a thundering good lift, you will say, for a settler in his second year only.

"But Karl's grass was not to be compared with what we get on our clearings. In the first place, the land was poor, and the seed did not take so well; then, he had sown rather scantily, so that a good deal of fern and flax and ti-tree came up with the young grass, and made it patchy and poor. Still, it was a great thing for these parts, where there is no native grass, for it enabled Karl to run sheep at once.

"Of course the grass was not all in one piece. It ran in and out among the standing bush, occupying the lower levels of ranges and the rising grounds at the bottom of gullies, spreading altogether over a good stretch of country. Karl got up sheep to stock it, but his capital was exhausted; and he ran into debt both for the sheep themselves, and with the shipper who brought them up. Not that this seemed of much consequence, for a year or two's increase of wool and lambs would pay off the debt and leave something in hand. But the Maori help he had didn't last very long; and as his creditors, being poor men, pressed him a good deal, Karl had to come into Auckland and raise money on mortgage.

"Land was low enough in value all over the colony, at that time, and a block up this way was not thought much of, you may be sure, so that Karl only got enough, by mortgaging his whole six thousand acres, to pay off his two creditors and leave him a very small balance. Well, the prospect was good enough, as any one but a new-chum can see, but all hung upon the sheep. There did not seem a great risk, but still there always is a certain amount of that with sheep. Disease did not trouble Karl much; there need be no great fear on that account in this country, if a little care be taken. Drought, too, was no matter for anxiety, as the land was sufficiently well-watered. But it was out of the question to fence in the grass, so we had to take what chance there was of the sheep straying, or of the damage wild pigs might do to the young turf, or of dingoes.

"Ah! you may laugh, but dingoes were what we feared most then. It has been proved by this time that if ever dingoes or runaway curs did exist, they are practically a myth, as far as this part of the island is concerned. Still, that was not so sure in those days, and the suspicion that they were in the bush was always a source of trouble to sheep farmers. The pigs' ravages we could check by a thorough hunt once or twice a year; and there was not much to fear from the sheep's straying, as, except one or two particular breeds, they will not go far into the bush or away from the grass. But the wild dogs were a different matter, if they came, and no one could be quite sure that any night might not find them among the flock.

"Such was the position of affairs when I came to live with Karl. Stop! I am forgetting one circumstance, the most important, in fact; for, if it had not been for her, I don't believe Karl would have cared so much about his farm. He was just the sort of man who is perfectly indifferent to ruin if it comes, so far as he himself is concerned; but she made his views of the future entirely of another colour.

"When loitering about Auckland, while he was getting his mortgage arranged, Karl got introduced to one or two families. He was not what you would term a society man, but, for all that, he managed to make up to a certain young lady he met. They fell in love with one another and got engaged, with all the usual rapidity of such affairs out here. There was even some talk of an immediate marriage, but the lady's father would not hear of that when he came to know Karl's position. He did not oppose the match in any way, but only stipulated for its postponement until Karl should have paid off his mortgage, and built a house more suitable for a family man than his then existing shanty. So Karl, inflamed with as violent a passion as I ever saw in any man, had to wait, three years as he calculated, until he was in a really proper condition to marry. This was a tremendous incentive to him to go ahead with vigour.

"When Karl returned to the bush I came with him, and took up my residence as one of the party at Hapuakohe. Besides myself Karl had one other chum, and there were two Maori boys who were generally on the farm, and who gave a good deal of labour in exchange for somewhat indefinite wages. They were yet unsophisticated in those days, and were not so fully aware of the pecuniary value of their own labour and time as they are now. Of course our work was hard and continuous. Looking after the sheep, especially at lambing time, and shearing them when the season came round, was the principal item. Then there was occasionally some job or other with the little herd : half a dozen cows, a bull, and a few young beasts, who roamed over bush and grass as they pleased, and had to be got up sometimes, or some trifling dairy work done. Then there were the usual garden crops, and the pigs to be seen to. Besides this, one of us had to row and sail the whole fifty miles down to Helensville every now and then, since there was no nearer place then where we could have obtained our stores.

"Nearly six months of the year we were hard at work falling bush and making new grassed clearings. We made no attempt at fencing, for Karl considered that the acquisition of more grass for his rapidly increasing flock was of paramount importance. Getting material, and fencing the Hapuakohe grass in, would indeed have been a stupendous task for our three pairs of hands to undertake, owing to the straggling character of the cleared land, and the consequent extent of the lines of fence required; moreover, there was no real necessity for it on a mere sheep-walk. The sheep would not stray very much, and, as Karl said, the only other reason was the dingoes, and no fence we could construct would have kept them out. But Karl had made great inquiries in Auckland, and from the natives, about these alleged wild dogs. He had not only been unable to find any one who had ever seen one, but even any one who knew any other person that had. So we almost succeeded in banishing the thought of them from our minds.

"Thus a couple of years passed away, and Karl's wool sales enabled him to bank a small instalment towards paying off his mortgage. However, it was evident that more than another year must elapse before he was in a position to marry, for the wages paid to the other man and I, together with current expenses, cost of more grass seed, and so forth, ate into the realized sum very deeply. On the other hand, the large annual increase of the flock would make the returns of each succeeding year very much greater. But I must tell you of our other chum, since it was about this time that Karl killed him.

"Ah! I thought that would startle you and fix your attention. Yes, there's a murder in my tale, coming presently. Listen!

"Brail, his name was; the only name I ever knew him by. He was a short, thickset man, a beggar to work, no matter what he was at. He professed to be English, but there was evidently some foreign blood in him, for his skin was darker than ours. His black bristling beard came up nearly to his eyes, and gave him a formidably ferocious look. He was reserved and silent, though civil enough to me in a general way. I gathered little by little, and at various times, that there was a bond of old standing between Karl and this man. Though he was a paid labourer, just as I was myself, yet it seemed that they had known one another for years. It could hardly be friendship as that is ordinarily understood; for Brail was a disagreeable companion at the best of times, and he and Karl were for ever snapping and snarling at each other. I concluded that the latent savagery which was in each, though differently manifested, formed a sort of tie between them.

"This Brail had a sullen hang-dog expression, and, at times, a fierce gleam in his scowling eyes that I did not like. Neither did Tama-te-Whiti, the old Maori chief, who was my very good friend in those days, as he has ever remained since. Tama used to visit Hapuakohe sometimes, and I well recollect his aversion for Brail. After speaking with him, Tama would often turn to me with an expression of profound contempt, and hiss out, 'kakino tangata!' I never really knew anything of the former relations of Karl and this man. I formed a theory from various little things that reached me, which may be true or may not. I imagine that Brail had been a convict, possibly a runaway and bushranger in Australia; that Karl, induced by some old-time regard for him, had aided him to escape to New Zealand, and had found him an asylum with himself. Something like this seems probable.

"Brail possessed a dog, which I must specially mention. It was one of those big yellow, shaggy-haired curs that are of the original Maori breed. This beast was trained into a very fair sheep-dog, and did its work along with the colleys belonging to the farm. It was the one thing upon earth that Brail seemed really to love, but even in this he showed his half-barbarous nature; for he would sometimes beat and kick the poor cur in the most brutal way, and again would caress and fondle it like a child. Whatever he did to it the dog never left him. It could scarcely be called obedient, but night or day, waking or sleeping, it never left its master. The animal was intelligent enough, and had that curious likeness to Brail that one may notice a dog often gets for its master. But he prided himself that the dog had some tincture of human nature in it. He had bought it, when a year old, from a Maori woman, at the price of two plugs of tobacco; and it seems that this woman had suckled the whelp herself, in its early infancy, having lost a new-born child of her own. You know that this peculiar custom of giving suck to young puppies is not an uncommon thing among Maori women. Brail's dog, as you will see by-and-by, had certainly acquired some super-canine qualities, but whether from its human foster-mother or from the teachings of its master, I cannot tell.

"Karl was indifferent to the beast. He was a hard man, and a rough one with all animals. He had no love or tenderness for them; nor did they show attachment to him. His own dogs obeyed him as their master, but did not love him as their friend. He cherished his sheep, looking on them as valuable property, without any feeling for them as living things. It is a character common in the bush. And this made a frequent cause for squabbles between him and Brail. Not that Brail cared for animals a bit more than Karl did, in a general way; only for that yellow dog of his. Though he often ill-treated it himself, it made him savage to see any one else do so; and Karl rarely came near it without a kick or a blow, more to tease Brail, I think, than for any other reason.

"All this time Karl used to make excursions down to Auckland as often as he could, to see his lady-love. He was getting more and more hopeful about his prospects; and would frequently talk about them to me, and about her also. But he never spoke on these topics before Brail; and I could see that he began to have thoughts of getting rid of the coarse, ill-mannered, foul-tongued ruffian, before he brought his bride up to the place. As it was, Brail rarely left the run. When he did go down to Helensville, or across to Whangarei, he invariably indulged in heavy drinking at the stores. He would fight and brawl with any sawyers or gum-diggers that might be hanging about; so that 'Karl's black devil of a chum' was no welcome sight at either settlement. And Karl was becoming more fastidious, as intercourse with his betrothed refined and softened his character.

"One day Karl, in entering the shanty, stumbled over the great carcase of the yellow dog, as it lay stretched out upon the floor. He kicked it savagely, and the brute turned and snapped at his leg; though his tall boots prevented the bite from doing him any harm. However, Karl, being enraged, seized an axe or something that was standing near and made a blow at the cur. But Brail rushed forward and seized his arm, and with one of his usual oaths growled out—

"'Can't you leave that dog alone? I tell you there'll be a row one of these times!'

"The two glared at one another silently for a moment, and then Karl, still heated, threw down the axe and, laughing lightly, said—

"'Oh no, there won't; because I'm going to give up both you and the cur!'

"'What?' cried Brail, and his teeth set, while an ashen pallor overspread his face, and his eyes seemed drawn in under his heavy lowering brows.

"Karl looked at him, and then seemed vexed, as though he had said something more than he intended.

"'There,' he said hastily, 'don't put yourself out. I merely meant that you'd better look for work somewhere else soon, as I intend altering things a bit.'

"'Oh, that's all, is it?' returned Brail, looking relieved. 'It's well it is all you meant, you know!' and with that he went out. Karl followed him, and some more passed between them that I did not catch. But there was a wicked look about Brail that I did not admire.

"Nothing further came of the incident; both men seemed to have forgotten it when next they met. Only a day or two after, as we were working together, Brail addressed a series of rather curious remarks to me. It never struck me at the time, but afterwards I thought he must have been trying to find out whether Karl had told me anything of his—Brail's—past history. I did not know anything of it then, and so Brail seemed satisfied.

"It was a custom of ours for one or two to camp out sometimes, when working on a distant part of the farm, so as to save two or three miles tramp backwards and forwards every morning and evening. So, after this, Brail built himself a hut in a little gully some three miles distant from the shanty. There were some lambing ewes lying on the grass in that direction, and Brail had to watch these, while falling bush on one side of the gully at the same time. So he moved up to his hut, carrying his necessaries along with him, and accompanied by his dog.

"Perhaps a fortnight after Brail had been camping up there, I was milking some of the cows near the shanty towards evening. While so occupied, I heard Karl's coo-ee from the direction of Brail's camp, where I knew he had gone. I answered, and presently the signal—three short quick coo-ees— informed me I had to go to him at once. I coo-ee'd the answer that I was coming, finished my milking, took the cans into the shanty, and set out. I ran up along the range, and had got more than half-way towards Brail's clearing before I saw anything of Karl. I was in an ill temper at having to go so far, being tired with the day's work, and so it never struck me that anything might be wrong.

"Presently I saw Karl sitting on a log, and as I made towards him, he rose and walked to me. I noticed there was blood on his shirt and pants, but that simply made me conclude that he had killed a sheep, and that I was summoned to help carry the mutton home before the flies could get to it. I merely said crossly—

"'Well, where is it?'

"Karl pointed towards Brail's camp without speaking, and we both walked on. Presently he spoke, in such hoarse, shaky tones, that I turned and looked closely at him. There was trouble and distress in his face of an unusual sort.

"'Old man,' he said, 'you'll stand by me, won't you?'

"'Of course,' I answered.

"'Are Wi and Tara back?' he asked then, meaning our two Maori boys, who had been away at their own village for several days. I replied in the negative, whereat he responded with a fervent 'Thank God!'

"'What's up?' I ejaculated in wonder.

"'I've killed Brail!' he whispered hoarsely.

"'Good God!' I cried. 'What do you mean, Karl?' and I sat down involuntarily; for the announcement came almost like a blow. He stood beside me, evidently deeply agitated.

"'Look here, old man! You're a true chum, I know. You'll keep this matter dark, for my sake —for *her* sake, rather. See here, I swear to you it was justifiable—nay, it was accident!'

"I simply nodded. He went on—

"'I went down to where he was at work without a thought of this; that I swear before Almighty God. Then that beast of his, that damned dog, flew at me. I raised my axe to strike at it. He came forward with that fierce rage on him that you may have noticed sometimes. I heard him grind his teeth and hiss between them, "You will have it then; you! the only man who knows my secret, b—— you!" And then he rushed at me with his knife in hand. I hardly know how it happened. I struck at him with the axe, meaning to knock the knife out of his hand. That was all I had in my mind, I take God as my witness—it was all. But somehow, I know not how, the axe caught him on the head. It was sharp, it was heavy; it cut through the bone as through the rind of a gourd. He fell—dead!'

"Karl spoke in hoarse, hurried, spasmodic tones. He wrung my hand in his, and looked beseechingly into my eyes.

"'Old man, you and I can share this—secret! You know me; you know I would not lie to you, not even for my life. You can believe the truth as I have told it you.'

"I waved his hand away, then took and wrung it hard. There was no need for more. I knew the man, I knew what he wanted of me. I understood at once. It was not fear for himself, it was for her, his wife that was to be. He had little cause to fear, indeed, for, with such evidence as I must perforce have given, no jury would have convicted him of more than manslaughter. But, why make the matter public at all? No one knew of it, except us two. No one need know of it. The shock of such a thing would be terrible for the innocent girl he hoped to marry. It might, probably would, break off the match.

"All this flashed across my mind. I had been in wild, lawless countries; I had seen many a violent death; it was no new and terrible thing to me. Boys! what would you have done? I liked Karl; I loved him, I think. We were friends; and the dead man I had detested. I believed every word he had said, as I believe it still. What need for more? Should I be the one to destroy all his future hopes, just for the sake of blurting about this miserable affair, to serve no particular end that I could see? No!

"I put my hands on poor Karl's shoulders, and looked him steadily in the face.

"'Come,' I said, 'let us put this thing out of sight, and—forget it.'

"He grasped my hands in his, while the tears

that welled from his eyes betrayed the depth and extent of his feelings. Then we went to where the body lay. I fetched a spade from the hut, and, under the shadow of some stretching fern-trees, in a secluded nook deep in the heart of a bit of bush that neither axe nor fire was ever likely to touch, we dug Brail's grave.

"We scarcely spoke at all. There was no need for words, for each of us understood the other so well. When I stripped the body bare, preparatory to laying it in its final resting-place, Karl simply nodded. He knew, without my telling him, why I did so. He comprehended that, in after time, if those bones were ever laid bare, there would be no vestiges of clothes or tell-tale buttons to give a clue to the remains. It might be supposed, in such a case, they were those of some slain warrior of Ngatewhatua or Ngapuhi.

"And then we gathered together every fragment of the dead man's property, and laid the things in his hut, and heaped up dead wood and dry brush, and set fire to the pile, and watched the bonfire blaze to ashes. And we scattered the ashes in a raupo swamp, and quietly went home.

"Anxious we were for some time after, but there was little reason for us to be so. The Maoris knew that Brail had intended leaving, and were not surprised when we said he had gone. I myself had conveyed a message from him to the storekeeper at Helensville, stating that he was looking for another job. What easier than to tell them there that he had swagged it through the bush to the east coast settlements? What simpler than to answer inquiries for him in that direction, by saying he had gone south? But no one ever cared to make close inquiry after him. The few who knew him did not like him. Poor wretch! ruffian as he was, I felt some pity for him; he, lying buried in the bush, friendless, unloved except by a dog as unlovable as he had been himself.

"As regards that dog, Karl had told me he had killed it, though he seemed somewhat confused about the matter when I thought of it and questioned him. He said that, after he had struck down Brail, his mind was so overwhelmed with the sudden horror of the affair, that he only faintly recollected what followed immediately. He fancied the dog attacked him; at any rate, he was sure he had chopped at it or stabbed it with his knife, and he distinctly remembered throwing its dead carcase to one side. So the matter was dismissed, it being merely a passing matter of surprise to me that I had not noticed the dog's body at the time. Yet I felt no call to go and look for it subsequently.

"Months flew by, and the thought of the unlucky affair was becoming less and less burdensome to us. Shearing time had come and gone, and the Maoris and one or two men from the settlements, who had come up to help us with it, had departed. Karl went down to Auckland in the cutter he had chartered to transfer the season's wool there. It would be the first time he had seen his betrothed since Brail's death. Ever since then he had been moody and depressed in spirits, melancholy and unlike himself. But the soft feminine influence had a vast soothing power over his mind, and he returned to Hapuakohe cheerful and happy. Care seemed no longer to weigh him down.

"Indeed, the prospect was brightening considerably for him. Wool was up in price; and Karl had not only paid the interest on his mortgage, but had now a good sum in bank towards paying off the principal. There were now between two and three thousand sheep on his clearings, and, barring accidents, another year ought to see him a free man and able to marry. I, too, participated in the good fortune that seemed to be with us, for I each year took the bulk of my wages in sheep, continuing them on the run with Karl's, on the usual system of half gains half risk.

Karl was never weary of talking to me of his

future wife; about his love for her, and hers for him; and we even ventured on castle-building by the fireside of nights. The new house was planned, its site fixed on, and the cost of it reckoned up. All the free happy life that was to be we talked over in pleasant anticipation. I was to get a place of my own and marry, too. But there! You know the sort of talk when times are good.

"One night we were sleeping as usual, in our bunks on opposite sides of the shanty. The fire was out, but the moon shone brightly through many a chink and crevice in the walls and roof. Suddenly I was awakened by a terrific scream from my chum. Hastily throwing off my blanket, I leapt out of the bunk and looked across at him. He was standing in the centre of the floor, the sweat pouring from his face and chest, his hair wet with it, his eyes starting, and his whole form shaking so that he could hardly keep erect.

"'Karl!' I cried, 'for Heaven's sake, what is it?'

"My voice seemed to bring him to himself, and, after I had got him a drink of cold tea, he became calmer, and was able to talk.

"'My God! I've had a fearful dream!' he said.

"'A nightmare, I suppose?' responded I.

"'I don't know," he returned; 'it was something more frightful than I ever experienced before. So horribly real, too.'

"After a while he continued—

"'I thought that Brail stood before me, just as he did that day when I—when I—killed him. His face had a detestably evil look, and he menaced me with his hands. I seemed to hear him say, "My vengeance is to come!" Then his form gradually changed into that of his big yellow dog, with fangs like a dragon's, and eyes that burnt horribly. It seemed to take the shape of a devil's face, springing at me out of hell, and I heard a confused sound of "Blood for blood!" Then the horror of it forced me to scream and awake.'

"Of course I affected to laugh at Karl's dream; one always does that with the victims of nightmare, I'm sure I don't know why, for there's nothing laughable about such things when you come to think of it. However, I discoursed in light fashion about the effects of imagination, disordered stomachs, and heavy suppers, though I saw all that I said had no particular effect on his mind. By-and-by we turned in again, and I slept till morning without further disturbance.

"When morning came I found that the dream still weighed heavily on Karl's spirits. He seemed to be possessed of the idea that it 'meant something,' though precisely what he could not say. He was downhearted and anxious, and his thoughts naturally turned to the sheep. They meant so much to him, poor fellow! He proposed that we should both make a thorough tour of the run, and asked me to catch a couple of horses that we might the better do so. For we had a few 'scrubbers' about the place, finding them necessary as economizing our time and strength in getting about the extensive farm.

"We set off after breakfast, Karl riding along the top of the range and I along the bottom, with the dogs following us as of course. The first gully, the same in which the shanty stood, had nothing to show us. The sheep on the clearings in it were feeding about as usual. But when we crossed over the range, and came in view of the wide basin on the other side, where was nearly five hundred acres of grass, we were surprised to find no sheep at all visible. We traversed it in all directions, sending the dogs round all the standing bush, and then we crossed the further range into a gully where a narrow strip of pasture extended for some two miles. As we came out of a piece of bush into this, we perceived the sheep. They were not feeding about in scattered groups, as was usual, but were collected in one flock, huddled up together. Some were lying down, panting, and all looked distressed and scared. It was easy to see they had been driven, and that quite recently.

"Karl galloped down the slope immediately, but I reined in for a moment, looking to see if anything was visible to account for this. Then a shout from Karl made me hasten to join him. He had dismounted, and was kneeling beside a ewe that lay prostrate on the hill-side. As I came up he looked at me with a terrible despair in his eyes, and, pointing to the sheep, said quietly—

"'That is what my dream meant. Look!'

"I jumped down and examined the ewe. It was dead; and the mangled throat and torn wool plainly told the cause.

"'Wild dogs!' I ejaculated with a bitter curse.

"We remounted and rode slowly about the clearings, narrowly observing the condition of the flocks. We found seven-and-thirty sheep dead or dying, the work of the dog or dogs on the previous night. A good many more were apparently injured from the driving. We made every possible search for the beasts that had done this, but not a trace of them was discoverable.

"Karl seemed overwhelmed by the disaster. A dark superstition seemed to have come over him, and to its influence he despairingly succumbed. Notwithstanding that, however, the innate courage of the man impelled him, now and to the end, to strive with every nerve against the evil fate that was pursuing him. Though he despaired from the first, unnecessarily, as I thought, he was not the sort of man to sit still with his hands in his pockets. No, he would fight to the last. We discussed what was possible to be done that day as we surveyed the slaughtered sheep. Karl croaked gloomily—

"'There is little use doing anything, however. There is the hand of God, or of the devil, I know not which, in this. It is a judgment on me—come from Brail's grave. Through a dog I came to kill him, by a dog his vengeance comes upon me!'

"'Bosh!' said I, 'you are letting that nightmare of yours ferment in your mind. What we've got to do is not to go fancying a pack of nursery tales, but to set about exterminating these brutes before they do more damage.'

"And then a thought struck me. I continued—

"'By the way, you're quite sure you killed that yellow dog?'

"'Certain,' was his emphatic reply.

"I took occasion, as we were riding near the place, to go and make a thorough search for the skeleton of the dog. I could not find it, however, though the thick undergrowth about there might certainly have hidden it all the while. But this satisfied me; I took up an unreasoning notion that

Brail's beast was the sheep-killer, though I could not attempt to account for why it had never been seen by us, if it were still living. I thought Karl might easily have been mistaken in his agitation, in thinking he had killed it; though why it should have disappeared for nearly a year, and then suddenly and mysteriously started on a career of crime, was beyond me. Perhaps it had gone mad in solitude; perhaps Brail's idea of its possessing half-human attributes by right of its peculiar nurture, might have something in it. The dog might have learnt a species of rascally cunning from its master. I did not know; I do not now. Doubtless these thoughts did not all enter my mind at that time, but have matured since. There is a weird and uncanny feature in the whole thing that I cannot explain. I simply relate the facts as I know them, without trying to explain the unexplainable."

Here, Old Colonial paused, and lit his pipe meditatively. We, knowing his hatred of interruptions, said nothing, and presently he took up the thread of his yarn again.

"So we drove the sheep that night upon the clearings in the home gully, and kept watch over them. But we knew we could not keep them there long, because of their number, and the scantiness of the feed at that season. Next day, Karl proceeded to lay poisoned meat about the run; while I rowed up the river to Tama-te-Whiti's kainga. I told the news to the Maoris, and Tama, with a score of his men, accompanied me back to Hapuakohe.

"We feasted the Maoris that night upon the slaughtered mutton, and held a great talk upon what should be done. In the morning we sallied forth to commence a systematic hunt through the surrounding bush, the natives being delighted to engage in this, especially as there was a prospect, unfortunately, of unlimited fresh mutton. To our horror, we found that the enemy had been at work again on the preceding night, and many more sheep were killed and crippled. This gave us a fresh impulse, and we went at the hunt with a will. Separating into four parties, under the respective leadership of Karl, Tama, myself, and another Maori, we mapped out the country before us to be carefully traversed. Every piece of bush, every swamp and possible shelter that lay in our way did we thoroughly beat. The clearings were examined, the dead sheep looked to, and every attempt was made to find traces of the dingoes; but when night brought the day's work to a close, we had all been entirely unsuccessful. Not the smallest trace of the wild dogs had been seen; only some of the bush-pigs had been found and a few killed incidentally.

"It is needless for me to continue in detail. For nearly a fortnight after, the same complete want of success persevered with us. In vain we scoured the bush far and wide by day, in vain we lay out watching all night, in vain we had recourse to every stratagem that our united cunning could devise. The result was always the same. Nothing rewarded our almost frantic efforts. And almost every night, under our very noses so to speak, frightful ravages were committed among the flocks.

"There was something so strange and uncommon about these night attacks, something so weird in our inability to obtain even a glimpse of the perpetrators, that the superstitious fancies of the Maoris began to come into play. I was getting nervous about Karl, for he was gloomy and abstracted, as well he might be, poor man! I alone knew he was imagining things and regarding himself as the victim of a dead man's vengeance. I knew that each fresh loss among the sheep went to his heart like a knife, for it seemed to divide him further from wedded happiness. Despair appeared to weigh him down more and more heavily. I began to fear for his reason.

"The intelligence of our misfortune was spreading through the country. Our Maori friends had augmented in number, coming from Tanoa and Matakohe and all round. The cordial kindness and brotherhood of the bush rushed in sympathy towards us. From Helensville came a boat-load of such necessaries as it was thought we should stand most in need of, with word to say that men would follow. The rough bushmen on the Wairoa sent to say they would come to our assistance if we needed them. The generous settlers of Whangarei sent word that they were coming in a body, to help us hunt down the dingoes, or to put up fences and pens for us, that Karl might pay for when he could, or not, it did not matter.

"All this simple self-sacrificing kindness touched us deeply, but it failed to rouse my poor chum's spirits.

"'It is no use,' he murmured. 'I am doomed to ruin. A third of the flock is gone already. The rest will follow. *She* can never be mine now.'

"'Stuff!' I replied to him. 'Rouse yourself, man. Do not despair yet. Come, we have work to do. Let us first of all settle these damnation curs!'

"'I am with you there! I am with you there!' he answered, his eyes glittering fiercely, as he rose and grasped his gun.

"Then came a night I remember well. I lay with Tama and some five or six Maoris in the bush on the top of a range, that overlooked a wide stretch of grass in the gullies on either side below us. The night was balmy and moonlit, for it was near Christmas time, and I was wearied, so I slept. Around us in the distance sparkled the camp-fires of the other watchers. Presently I was roused by Tama, who, in an excited whisper, bade me listen. I peered forth from the edge of the jungle, and could hear a low, dull, rushing sound. I knew what that meant. It was a large flock of sheep, running hard. In a moment they came into view out of the shadows, heading straight for where we crouched, plainly visible in the flood of moonlight that streamed upon the open side of the range. I could hear the quick breathing of the Maoris beside me, as I leant forward keenly intent upon the flock, my gun ready in my hands. I watched the flock as it streamed rapidly along the hill-side, and saw that here and there, in its track behind, lay single sheep, crippled by stumps or holes in the ground, or, as I knew by experience, with mangled throats that spoke of the fangs of murderous brutes. We waited and watched, the moonlight gleaming on the barrels of our ready guns. The flock passed close below us, tearing along in the utmost extremity of panic. And our levelled weapons were ready.

"As I am a sinful sinner, what I tell you is the

plain unvarnished truth. As the flock passed below our eyes, we saw no beast of any kind but sheep. No dog was visible there, that I could swear to. And yet, close before us, a fine fat wether suddenly leapt up and dropped, so near that we could see the fresh blood spurting from a wound in its throat. I rushed out upon the clearing and looked at it; I looked after the vanishing flock and all around me, but no sign of the destroyer could I see. A horrible thrill passed all through me, for this was something mysterious, unnatural, and unnerving. I could not resist the sudden shivery feeling that crept over me at this most unaccountable occurrence.

"And then, from close beside me, rose Tama's shrill coo-ee. Louder and louder it rang out into the still night, till answers came pealing from the camps on the ranges around us. After a little we saw the other watchers coming to us from their various posts on the run, until presently all were collected together, a silent wondering group—a hundred Maoris, and Karl and I. Then Tama spoke. What he said I do not know. It was some vague relation of what we had seen, together with frequent references to the 'tahipo'—devil—and some 'kararehe tahipo'—demon dog. But the wild excitement of the chief, the deadly terror that possessed him, soon infected all the others. They gathered round him in an eager cluster, and the deep 'Ai,' and 'kuia' that broke from one and another, testified their earnest attention and concurrence.

"Then they knelt down, there on the grass around the dead wether. It was a curious group we made in the moonlight on the hill-side, just beyond the shadows of the bush. And Tama lifted up his voice—literally so—and prayed. He prayed through the Lord's Prayer, and the Creed, and through half the questions and answers of the Catechism beside. Being agitated, no doubt, he scarcely knew exactly what he was saying. And then it seemed to me, as well as I could follow the Maori, that he indulged in an extempore delivery, half prayer, half incantation, to meet the special requirements of the case.

"When this performance, so grotesque yet so simply serious, was over, these half-savage Christians rose and began to take leave of us. They could not stay to fight devils, they said; God and his angels could alone do that, and they had prayed that it might be so. Many blubbered as they shook hands with us; they would have willingly fought for us with anything of flesh and blood, but terror of the unseen had now overmastered their sympathy. They hurried away over the range and down to the beach where their canoes lay, and so, flying from haunted Hapuakohe, they left us two alone.

"All this could not fail to have its effect on one's mind. I felt very uncomfortable, but Karl seemed to take everything as though he had expected it. When daylight came, and I was able to reason more calmly about the mystery, I thought I saw a possible solution. It was evident there could not be several dogs, or we must have seen them, or traces of them. Probably there was only one, for, great as was the havoc that had been wrought, I did not think it was impossible for a single ferocious beast to have caused it. And then I reflected that a dog might look so like a sheep in the moonlight, as not to be readily detected among a flock. Why, I remembered that a shaggy, grayish-yellow cur, such as Brail's dog had been, for instance, was positively indistinguishable amid a flock of sheep at night, especially when the moon was shining. But the extraordinary cunning and careful scheming that seemed apparent in this case were, I confess, beyond my powers to fathom; nor have I been able to account for them to this day.

"We did what we could, we two, while we waited for the promised help from the settlements. You might think we could have shepherded the flock near the shanty, and guarded them with our dogs;

but that we had found to be impossible. First, grass was scarce there, and we had, of course, no other feed to give them. Then, they had got so wild with the constant chasing, that we must have been continually worrying them with our own dogs, which would only have made matters worse. There was literally nothing to be done, but to watch for and kill the dingo.

"Oh! it was a piteous sight to see the dead sheep lying scattered about the clearings. And among the survivors there were so many hurt that must die, so many more that were injured so as to be practically valueless; for the chasing on the rough, stump-covered hill-sides had done more damage than the actual fangs of the wild dog. I was myself a sufferer, but my loss was as nothing to poor Karl's. He, I saw, was ruined, if not irretrievably, at least for some years to come. But this made his marriage impossible now, unless the lady's parents took a very different view of things. Surely, I thought, the news must by this time have got to Auckland. Perhaps the father had already resolved to break off the match in consequence. I was only a plain, simple bush-farmer, and it seemed to me that if this girl were true in her love for Karl, she would certainly leave her father and come to him in his trouble. I thought I would myself write and tell her to do so, for, you see, I feared that he would go melancholy mad for loss of her. But the end of it was come."

Again Old Colonial paused, and gazed intently into the fire, with a sad, grave expression shadowing over his usually jolly, sunburnt face.

"I left my camp one morning and strolled across the run to the place where Karl had been watching. He had selected the top of a steep bluff that jutted out into the river and that, on the landward side, overlooked a great extent of the run. As I climbed up the range I shouted to him repeatedly, but, as there was no answer, I concluded he was sleeping, and so walked quietly on till I came out on the top. There were the smouldering remains of his fire, the billy in which he had boiled his tea, his blanket lying as he had left it, but Karl himself was not there. I shouted again and looked about me, and then something made me start.

"It was his gun lying on the ground. I picked it up, and saw that it had been discharged. There was blood upon the stock, and stuck to the hammer was a wisp of coarse yellow hair. Amazed, and filled with a sudden cold sensation of fear, I examined the ground about me. I saw grass and bushes trampled and broken as though there had been a struggle on the spot. I saw splashes and blots of blood here, there, and everywhere. And then something prompted me to look over the cliff. What I saw nearly caused me to fall, so horribly did my heart leap in my throat. Down below there, on the cruel rocks, head downwards on the beach, lay his body. Dead he was, you could see that from the top. Poor Karl!

"I rushed down through the gully on the left, and made my way to where he lay. His head was broken by the fall, but there were horrible wounds besides upon his throat and limbs, gaping, torn, and deep, too plainly the marks of some fierce beast's teeth. And as I knelt beside the body, weeping, stupified, agonized by the horror of the thing, a fancy crept into my poor brains that I had been a witness of that scene upon the bluff the night before; when nought but the moon was there to see, with the creek singing through the bush in the gully, and the river-tide sweeping along below.

"I fancied I saw him sitting moody and despairing by the fire. And up through the thick jungle of the gully comes stealing the great yellow body of that dreadful brute, that devilish cur that had first ruined him and now meant to kill him. I saw it spring upon him as he sat, with fangs gleaming and savage eyes of fire. I saw the flash of his gun, the swinging blow, the curse of the man, and the growl of the dog. I could fancy the ferocious joy upon the face of the half-maddened man as he grappled with his foe. I saw the hard, fierce struggle—glistening teeth opposed to flashing steel. And then I saw him conquer, but—only to seize the ponderous brute, to hurl it from the cliff far into the river, and, staggering, wounded to the death, overbalancing, to fall headlong himself.

"I was roused from this dream by the trampling of horses' feet. It was the men from Whangarei—kind, cheery, sympathetic souls. They had ridden all the way—all the fifty miles along the Maori track through the forest. Poor as they were, they had put aside their own concerns, and had come over to help us in our trouble.

"But they were too late—too late! except to help me lay my poor dead chum to rest.

"Ah! you guess now who the lady is that was our hostess at Hapuakohe the other day. Karl bequeathed to her, as a matter of course, all he had to leave. But she knows only a small part of what I have been telling you. There are portions of the tale that neither she nor her husband know aught of. You can guess what they are. Never hint at this story in their presence, or in that of their children. I know I can rely on your silence. Moreover, there is nothing to give rise to mention of it, for no sheep-worrying wild-dogs, or dingoes, have ever been heard of in the Kaipara since the day that Karl died.

"When we were over there, I took the opportunity of visiting the place where I laid him, long, long ago, as it seems to me now. A thicket of ferns hides all traces of the grave, and the wooden cross that marked it has fallen and decayed among them.

"What matter! He is at rest. And the kind trees that shadow round him scatter the golden kowhai bells and crimson pohutukawa blossoms upon his mossy coverlet. The tide flows at his feet, risping over the oyster-beds, swirling among the mangroves, hurrying to the distant sea; just as it did on that night so long ago, when it bore with it away through the moonlit forest—away in secret and unfathomable mystery—the accursed carcase of the Demon Dog."

CHAPTER VIII.

OUR LUCK.

THE sun has just risen, and brilliant gleams of light are playing upon the waters of the Firth of Thames. Above, in the air, rise the rugged summits of the mountains, that golden range which stretches down through Coromandel, from Cape Colville to Aroha, a hundred and twenty miles of El Dorado. And just before us, occupying a flat at the base of the hills, is the gold-field centre, Grahamstown.

The steamer which has brought us from Auckland, leaving late last night, is just drawing alongside the little wharf at Shortland, having, for some occult reason, passed by the long wooden pier that runs out into the stream a little lower down, at Grahamstown proper. She is loaded to the water's edge with a human cargo. There is hardly standing room aboard of her, though she is a fair-sized craft. Men crowd every available part of her. Men of all kinds—from the smooth-faced, sleek young clerk, clean as to linen, gay as to dress, fresh from the city atmosphere which has hitherto bounded his experience, up to the hirsute, sun-browned, rough-looking bushman, in jumper, moleskins, and ankle-jacks. There are men of various nationalities, and of every class, all eager, expectant, and excited, huddled together promiscuously, and all have talked through the whole weary night of but one subject —gold.

There is a "rush"; that is the explanation of the crowded steamer, of other crowded steamers and sailing-craft, that have come and will come, of men on horseback and men on foot, who are converging through the roadless country from all sides upon the valley of the Thames. A day or two hence, a new extension of the gold-field is to be proclaimed and opened. Rumour says the prospectors have struck a reef of unexampled richness; and almost every one in Northern New Zealand is burning with anxiety to be on the spot and take up a claim.

Our shanty has experienced the gold-fever, mainly through the influence of O'Gaygun. Things had not been very brisk with us of late, and so it was determined to take a temporary spell of gold-mining. All the community are partners in the enterprize, but only four of us are actually going on to the field. Old Colonial was not to be drawn away from the Pahi, and he, with some of the others, remains to carry on the farm. O'Gaygun, the Little'un, and the writer, are now landing from the steamer, while Dandy Jack, who preceded us, is already in Grahamstown.

You see, even gold-seeking requires some little capital to start one at it. Here, the mining is all in quartz, which necessitates it. There is no alluvial washing to enable one to pan out one's dust, and pay one's way with it from week to week. Now, it happened that we had scarcely any ready money, so we had to raise it. About a fortnight ago we chartered a schooner in the Kaipara, loaded her with fat steers, a few horses, some sheep, barrels of pork, sacks of potatoes, and other produce, and sent her off. She was to round the North Cape, and to run for the Thames, and Dandy Jack went with her. In anticipation of the coming rush, we reckoned that he would be able to sell all the cargo at a good figure, and have a tolerable sum in hand to carry us on when we took up our claim. Subsequently, we three others went down to Auckland, and took the steamer thence.

The crowd, slowly disgorged on Shortland wharf, turns to walk towards Grahamstown for the most part. The two places are one town now, being connected by a street about a mile long. Less than ten years ago Shortland was the original and only township, and then consisted of a single store, kept by a half-breed. The land was all owned by natives, and the stubborn old chief of the district, Te Moananui, could not be prevailed on to part with territory to the Pakeha.

Then came the discovery of gold; and at last government got a strip of land from the Maoris. It was opened as a gold-field on July 27, 1867. Messrs. Hunt, Cobley, Clarkson, and White are closely connected with the early history of the place. They were the original prospectors, and struck it rich. Though having scarcely money enough to buy tools with at the start, they made a princely fortune out of their claim.

Later, the Caledonian eclipsed even the enormous success of Hunt's claim, yielding no less than ten tons of gold during the first year. Some other claims have done well, and more, of course, have altogether failed. But the most money has been made on the Stock Exchange. Each claim is necessarily worked by a company, and some of its scrip is got into the market. A share may one day not be worth a five pound note, nay, has even been given for a day's board at an hotel; a month later a quarter of that share may change hands at £10,000.

This young town looks a good deal more than

its actual age. A good street runs right from Shortland to Grahamstown, and though there are gaps here and there, showing how close the untilled wilderness is to the pavement, yet the shops, the public buildings, the vehicles and foot-passengers, all evidence a settled town life. There are some short side-streets, neat houses and trim gardens; there is quite a nucleus at the Grahamstown end, where the principal batteries and crushing-mills are situated. There are ten churches and five banks, besides other public establishments in the place; for the borough has a resident population of over five thousand, and about as many more in the suburbs of Tararu and Parawai, and in the district of the gold-field generally. Such a rush as is now taking place must also largely augment the population.

We make straight for the Governor Bowen Hotel, for we are thoroughly ready for breakfast. There we meet Dandy Jack, calm as ever amid the stormy excitement that is raging all around, though a feverish glitter in his eye shows that inwardly he is as other men. He tells us that he has realized the cargo, but has not done so well with it as we had sanguinely expected. The Thames was better supplied with provisions than we supposed. Nevertheless, we have a fair sum in hand to make a start with.

Dandy Jack has kept the horses; he says we shall need them. It appears that the new field is twenty miles or so from here, in a district called Ohinemuri. The Warden is camped there, and will proclaim the gold-field two days from now. Not until that is done can any one take out the necessary permit to dig for gold. And then there will be a terrible race from the camp to the range where the prospectors' claim is situated; for every one, of course, will wish to peg out his claim as near as possible to that reserved for the original discoverers. It seems that every one is buying or stealing horses for this exciting event; and Dandy Jack has refused incredibly handsome offers, and kept the animals he so luckily brought here in order that we may have a chance of picking out a good claim.

It is settled among us that Dandy Jack and O'Gaygun shall at once start for the Warden's Camp. They will go by the native track through the bush, and will ride, of course. The other two horses they will lead, loading them with our tools and swag. The Little'un and I remain at Grahamstown, as we wish to see all we can of gold-mining there. We shall reach the new field in time for the reading of the proclamation, getting there by means of a steamer, that is already plying briskly up and down the river Thames.

After seeing off the two cavaliers and their pack-horses, the Little'un and I begin roaming about the settlement. By certain friendly offices we are enabled to visit various claims, among which are Hunt's, the Kuranui, the Caledonian, and the Golden Crown, of course. We have here opportunity for seeing all the methods employed for quarrying out the auriferous rock, and we get much valuable information, and many useful practical hints regarding geological strata, the lay of the quartz, the character and variations of gold-reefs, etc.

Then we visit the great pump, the principal feature of interest in Grahamstown, as it is, perhaps, the most stupendous enterprise in the colony as yet. Water had proved a source of much trouble in the Caledonian and other claims, which penetrated to some depth. An association was therefore formed for the erection of a pump. £50,000 was the cost of its erection, and as much more is being spent in sinking to lower levels.

The engine has a nominal force of 350 horse power. The cylinder is eighty-two inches in diameter, and the length of stroke ten feet. The pump pipes are twenty-five inches diameter; and the machine can raise ten tons of water per minute. Its operation already extends to a depth of four hundred feet below the sea-level. The output of the field, from 1867 to 1875, has been roughly estimated to have been 1,080,202 ounces, valued at £3,465,093.

The next objects of interest to us are the quartz-crushing batteries. Of these we are told there are thirty-six on the field. The smallest has four stampers, and the largest sixty-two. Most of them have between twenty and forty stampers.

We watch some of them at work; seeing the mighty pestles thundering down upon the blocks and fragments of stone, grinding them slowly into powder. We see tons and tons of hard shining quartz fed under the feet of the rows of stampers. Then we see the sandy dust into which the rock has been disintegrated, undergoing a washing to separate from it the minute particles of gold. We see it puddled up with water in great vats, and converted into a thin mud. We see this liquid sent over "beds," and "floors," and "ladders," and "blanketings," and washed again and again. Finally we see the gold that was in it collected as sediment from the various washings. Yellow heaps of it are piled in appointed places, waiting for removal. Then comes the final process, the refining with mercury and fire, and the casting of the gold into ingots.

Not all the batteries or claims are being worked,

for many of their crews are either gone or going to the new field. But this stoppage is merely temporary. After the fresh excitement has subsided, the men will come back to their work, finding that £2 10s. or £3 a week of wages is better than making nothing out of a claim of one's own.

So we see as much of the place as we can, even climbing up the rugged ranges, and from their wild summits looking down over the whole panorama of the gold-field, with the waters of the firth beyond it, and the bush-clothed heights upon the further shore. And then we find a novel interest in the *table d'hôtes* at the hotels, with the singularly mingled company assembled at them. Everywhere is a feverish excitement; everywhere every one can talk of nothing but the new Ophir that is so soon to be opened.

We even indulge in a game or two of billiards, a rare novelty and luxury to us bush-farmers of the Kaipara. And we gaze with admiration and reverence upon the well-displayed charms and attractions of the barmaids in the saloons.

One of these ladies, more affable and less assuming than her sisters, who are haughtily inflated with the deep reverence and homage of thirsty crowds of men, actually condescends to favour us with a few words of conversation. We are gratified and honoured beyond measure.

This most gracious lady informs us that the proprietor of her bar is about to erect an hotel on the new field, and that she is going up to tend bar there. But it appears that the glorious profession of which she is a member is not what it was. Certain regulations that mine-owners have lately made, anent the taking of "specimens" from the mines by the paid miners, have almost destroyed a poor girl's chances. She relates a legend about "the first barmaid" who appeared at Grahamstown, her predecessor at this very bar. That lady was the cynosure and magnet for countless courtiers, of course, and she would seem to have been a very practical and square-headed young woman. Her many admirers found that to gain a word, a look, a smile, a ravishment of whatever kind, it was needful to offer a frequent "specimen" for the lady's acceptance.

"She was dashing, you know, but not a beauty by any means," says our informant, with a toss of her be-chignoned head. After a few months, she sent a boxful of "specimens," the cherished donations of her hundred slaves, to be crushed at one of the batteries. They realized, so rumour hath it, some ten or twelve thousand pounds. And the fair one, satisfied with having blandished this pile out of the Thames, and probably finding her opportunities at an end, winged her triumphant flight back to England.

The gorgeous and bedizened beauty who treats us to this tale, hopes to do likewise at Ohinemuri. Her attractions are greater than those of the lucky princess she has been telling us about; or, no doubt, she secretly considers that they are. She hopes to see us at her new bar, and trusts we will remember to bring her a "specimen" now and then. This with a flash of black eyes, that makes the giant Little'un shiver with emotion in his number fourteen boots, and leaves us both helpless victims of the siren.

The afternoon of the next day finds us on board the river steamer, making our way to the spot where, as we fondly hope, fortune lies waiting for us. The steamer is cram full, of course, but the voyage is not to be a long one. Although the Thames river is navigable for nearly fifty miles, up to the base of Aroha Mountain, we have not got to go very far up it. Something under a score of miles separates the new gold-field from Grahamstown. Perhaps a dozen miles from the mouth of the river we enter its tributary, the Ohinemuri creek. The whole district around is known as the Ohinemuri Plains, being a portion of the lower valley of the Thames.

Our experience of the Grahamstown neighbourhood had led us to expect anything but a picturesque country. We are agreeably disappointed. The river winds through what are called plains here, but the term is only relatively applied. The "plains" are broken with spurs and undulations from the higher ranges that bound them, and the country is anything but one uniform level.

On either hand rise heavy mountainous ranges, sometimes receding far into the distance, sometimes approaching nearer to the river. Tracts of splendid forest clothe the country, interspersed with bare rock, open fern-land, low jungles of light scrub, marsh, and fen. Forest and mountain form a background to the broad valley through which winds the (really) silver Thames, abounding with fish, its low banks and firm sandy shores rich with a luxuriant shrubbery. Further up, every mile adds to the beauty of the scene around.

And all this great valley, containing a million acres doubtless, is as Nature made it, unmarred by the hand of man, save some little spots here and there, where Maori kaingas are situated, and that limited area which the gold-seeker now calls his own. It is easy to see that this must eventually become a magnificent expanse of farming tracts.

At present all this land is still owned by the

natives, a morose and sullen tribe. Great difficulty was experienced in getting the Grahamstown field out of their hands, and still more trouble has surrounded the acquisition by Government of the new extension. The chief, Te Hira, has been overruled by his counsellors, and has reluctantly consented to the sale of a portion of his territory. Already is he disgusted with the advent of the Pakeha, and talks of retiring with his chief adherents to some wilder solitude. But his sister, Mere Kuru, who holds equal dignity with himself, seems disposed to change her ancient habits. She is said to be even welcoming the new order of things, and is qualifying herself to become a leader of modern Maori fashionable society. She rules a large kainga, situated on the Ohinemuri creek, about midway between Cashell's and Paeroa, the two new landing-places for the gold-field.

At the latter place we disembark, and proceed at once to the Warden's camp, which is not far off. It is a scene of glorious confusion. Round about the tent of the official, with its flag, are grouped sundry other tents, huts, wharès, breakwinds of every conceivable kind, and of every possible material. It is dark now, as evening has descended, and the numerous camp-fires make a lurid light to heighten the wildness of the scene. Crowds of men are grouped about them, eating, drinking, singing, shouting, or talking noisily of the everlasting subject—gold.

Through the camp we pick our way, stumbling over stumps and roots and boulders, splashing into deep mud and mire, visiting every fire, and asking for the whereabouts of our chums. We begin to think we shall never find them amid the confusion of the wild, disorderly camp, and have some thoughts of applying for hospitality at the next fire. At length one man, whom we have asked, replies to our questions—

"Do you mean a pretty sort of chap, looking like a dancing-man or a barber, and a big, red-headed Irisher with him for a mate? They're over yonder, camped in Fern-tree Gully. Got some horses with 'em, yes!"

We thought this evidently must refer to Dandy Jack and O'Gaygun, so we stumbled down the little dell, and found our surmise was right. We were quickly welcomed, and supplied with supper.

Our friends had erected a rude breakwind of poles and fern-fronds, sufficient to shelter our party from the rain while we slept, should there be any. A huge fire blazed in front of it; while not far off, and well in view, the horses were tethered. They were secured in far more than ordinary fashion, with headstalls, and lariats, and hobbles. Dandy Jack said there was momentary fear of their being stolen, by miners anxious to use them on the momentous morrow, and it was even thought necessary for one of us to keep watch over them all night, which duty we performed by turns. There was little fear of anything else being plundered; indeed, next day we left our swag exposed on the ground without anything being taken. But horses meant odds in the coming lottery, and the most honest men were willing, just at that excited moment, to annex temporarily the first they came across.

At length morning comes, bringing with it the eventful day, the 3rd of March, 1875, which is to see the opening of the new field. From earliest dawn the camp is astir; and as the sun climbs the sky, so does the intense hubbub increase. Oh, for an artist's brush to delineate that scene! Pen and ink are far too feeble.

Men move about like swarming bees, eagerly talking and shouting with all and sundry. Groups are gathered here and there, their eyes one minute glancing anxiously towards the Warden's tent, the next moment looking out across the wooded plain, as it swims in the morning sunshine, towards the towering ranges in the distance, where an abrupt alteration in their outline shows the situation of the

Gorge, the spot where the prospectors' claim is known to be, the goal of every hope to-day.

No one dares to leave his horse now for an instant. Those that have any, like ourselves, for the most part remain mounted, restlessly circling about the camp. Every man that could beg, borrow, or steal it, appears to have got a riding-beast of some sort. A few are even bestriding bullocks, judging, probably, that in the general scrimmage and stampede, even those ungainly steeds will distance men on foot.

We are all equipped with everything immediately necessary, and are ready for the start. A tumultuous assemblage it is that is now moving in a perfect frenzy of excitement about the Warden's tent. A concourse of men—rough men and gentle men, blackguards and honest, young and old, ragged and spruce, grave and gay, but all fevered to their heart's core with the burning fury of the gold-digger.

Amid the throng there move a few Maoris from the neighbouring kainga. Queer, old, tattooed worthies, half-dressed in European rags, half draped in frowzy blankets. These are stolid, disdainful. They have come to see the Pakeha in their mad state. And there are others, younger men, smiling and chattering, evidently anxious to get excited, too, could they only understand what all the fuss is about. There is a contemptuous air about them, a kind of pity for the curious insanity that is rife among the Pakeha about them.

And now the wished-for hour approaches. A rude table is rigged up in front of the Warden's tent, at which clerks take their places. Two or three of the armed constabulary are visible, ostensibly to keep order, which it would take more than all the force to do. And a riotous throng of horsemen and footmen wrestle and struggle for front places near the table. Apparently, two or three thousand men are waiting eagerly for the word to start.

Then the Warden steps forth, looking grave and dignified in his official coat and cap. He is the only calm person present, and is received with vociferous exclamation by the crowd. He holds in his hand a roll of papers, which he proceeds at once to open, mounting a convenient stump by way of a rostrum. Then he commences to read—the Riot Act, one would say, looking at the seething, roaring mob around. In fact, it is the proclamation of the Ohinemuri gold-field, under the Mining Act of the colonial legislature. But no one can hear a word.

Presently the reading is done, the Warden lifts his cap with a smile, announcing that the field is open. A tumult of cheering breaks forth, and then every one rushes at the clerk's table, and, fighting and struggling for precedence, dumps down his note (£1) for the "Miner's Right," which is his license and authority to dig for gold within the limits of the field.

I cannot describe that fierce conflict round the table and tent; it is all confusion in my mind. It is a wild jumble of warring words, and furiously struggling shoulders and elbows, arms and legs. Somehow we get our licenses early, mainly owing, I think, to the stalwart proportions and weighty muscles of the Little'un and O'Gaygun. Out of the plunging crowd we fight and tear our way, duly armed with our "authorities." As does every one so do we, namely, fling ourselves on our horses' backs, and ride headlong across the country in the direction of the Gorge.

What a race that is! No run with a pack of English foxhounds could compare with it. Never a fox-hunter that dared have ridden as we rode that day, across a country so rough and shaggy. But our incitement is greater than ever fox-hunter had, for it is a frantic chase for wealth, with all the madness of gambling thrown into it. It is a race whose goal is gold!

There is no road, of course. Our way lies

across a country jungled with fern and scrub and bush. The ground is broken with abrupt descents and short but rugged rises. There are streams and marshes to be plunged through or jumped over. There are devious twists and turns to be made to avoid insurmountable obstacles. Scarce is there a track to show the way, merely the faintest indication of one cut through the wooded tracts by the surveyor's gang. And we have six miles and more to make, riding with frantic eagerness and reckless speed, conscious that two thousand men have entered for the race, and that only a few can win.

Thoroughly well mounted, and accustomed from our cattle-driving experiences to such rough riding as this, we four chums do justice to the start we managed to get. Not more than a score or so are ahead of us, and some of them we are overhauling.

There are dozens of casualties, of course. As we gallop along I see a man and horse go down, on the steep side of a gully. They roll over together, and together flounder to the bottom. The unlucky rider screams with pain, for his legs and ribs are broken, and calls to us to help him. We hesitate half a moment, but the gold-fever is on us, and we hurry on. At such a time humanity is dead, even in the most honourable breast. It is like a battle.

Again, Dandy Jack and O'Gaygun are in front of me. Before them rides a regular Thames miner, bestriding a lean and weedy horse of very poor description. It is easy to see, too, that he is not accustomed to the saddle, though he is urging his beast to its utmost, and doing all he knows to get on. We are coursing along the side of a slope, dense ti-tree jungle above and below us, and only a rough narrow way through it. The miner's horse ahead stumbles and trips, grows frightened, and becomes unmanageable, turning broadside on in the narrow path and blocking it.

I hear Dandy Jack and O'Gaygun shout in warning, but the miner has no time to get out of their way. Riding abreast they charge down upon him, utterly regardless of consequences. Over goes horse and man beneath the shock of their rushing steeds, and, a moment later, my nag leaps over the fallen and follows at their heels.

Oh, the rush and fury of that ride! My head still swims as I think of it. All sense of care is gone; all thought of risk or accident banished. A wild, mad excitement surges through every vein, and boils up within my brain. I only know that hundreds are hurrying after me, and before me there is a dazzle and glitter of gold. Who heeds the fallen, the vanquished, the beaten in the race?

Who cares for peril to life or limb? There is but one idea the mind can hold—on! on!

By-and-by, and when our panting, foaming horses seem utterly giving out, responding neither to voice nor spur, bit nor whip, we find ourselves within the Gorge. A splendid mountain scene is that, had we but time to look at it. We have not. Our worn-out steeds carry us wearily up and along the steep hill-side, beneath and among the trees that cast their umbrage all over the golden ground. Climbing, struggling, pressing ever onward, we pass the grim defile, and, in the wild and beautiful solitude of primeval nature, we find our goal.

Through the trees we spy a clearing, lying open and sunlit on the steep mountain-side. A clearing, hardly to be so designated, for it is merely a space of some few acres where fallen, half-burnt trees lie prostrate, jumbled in inextricable confusion with boulders, rocks, jutting crags, and broken mounds of fresh-turned soil and stone. A handkerchief upon a post, some newly-split and whitened stakes set here and there around the *débris*, the babble and vociferation of men, those who have got before us, around and about, all sufficiently proclaims that our race is at an end, and that this before us is the prospectors' claim.

There is no time to be lost, for many behind us

are coming on, and will be upon the ground a few minutes later. And more and more are coming, pressing onward from the rear with feverish ardour. We spring from our now useless steeds and hasten to select our ground. Above, and on each side, nay, even immediately below the prospectors' claim, those lucky first ones are already pegging out their lawful areas. Depending on certain indications that a hasty glance reveals, and on advice that Dandy Jack has previously received in mysterious confidence from one of the prospectors, we pass below the ground already seized, and there, a little to the right, we proceed to set up the stakes and clear the ground that we claim as ours.

As we proceed to make the dispositions which secure to us that which we have already named " O'Gaygun's Claim," the row and racket around rings fiercer over the mountain side. Parties of men are arriving every moment on the ground, and proceeding at once to map out rock and bush into squares and parallelograms, and to peg out their several claims. With the prospectors' claim for centre and nucleus, the area of the occupied ground momentarily increases. Above, around, below, we are hemmed in by earth-hungry gold-seekers, who each and all are greedy as starved tigers for their prey.

Not without many disputes is the work accomplished. Oath and remonstrance, angry quarrelling and bandying of words soon transform that peaceful fastness of nature into a pandemonium of humanity; and words give place to blows, as boundaries are fixed, and claims measured off. Fierce fights are waged over many an inch and yard of ground. The heated blood of the gold-seeker brooks little opposition, and I fear that even revolvers and knives are shown, if not used, between rival claimants.

Yet the hot fury of the rush subsides after a time, and each party proceeds to investigate what authority allows it, and to reconcile divisions with its neighbours. Fires are built and camps are formed, for no one dare leave his claim unoccupied, and preparations are made for a night more confused and uncomfortable than those previously spent at the Warden's camp.

Next day the work commences. The Warden and his aids register the claims and their respective owners. Parties are told off to cut and construct a road. Miners begin to build up huts and habitations, and to bring up from the river their swags, provisions, and tools. Trees fall beneath the axe; rocks are shattered and the ground disturbed with pick and spade; while pounding and panning, assaying and testing goes on vigorously. For no one knows exactly how the reefs will run, or where the richest stone will be found. Nor can that be more than conjectured until tunnelling has been carried to some depth. Most of the claims will prove abortive and valueless; only a few will yield paying quantities of gold; only one or two, perhaps, will bring wealth to their owners. We work and hope.

Three months later, what have been the results, and what are the prospects? I stand at the door of the rude hut we live in, and look abroad over the gold-field, pondering. It is evening, a memorable evening for us, as will presently appear. But we are depressed and down-spirited, for luck has not been with us. "O'Gaygun's Claim" is apparently one of the blankest of blanks in the lottery of the gold-field.

What a difference is apparent in the scene around from that it presented three months ago, when we rode here in wild excitement and hot haste. The grand and lonely Gorge is now populous with life. Trees have fallen beneath the axe, and even their stumps have altogether disappeared over a great extent. The wide hill-side has been riven and torn and excavated by pick and spade, and gaping tunnels yawn here and there. Houses and huts and tents have risen all around, and a rough young town now hangs upon the mountain's shoulder.

Newness and rawness and crudity are prevailing features of the place, yet still it begins to look like the abode and workshop of civilized men. Stores and hotels, primitive but encouraging, hang out their signs to view; and a road, rough but practicable, winds down across the lower ground to Paeroa, the river landing-place, where, too, another township is being nursed into existence. Down below a couple of crushing-mills are already set up and hard at work, belching forth volumes of smoke, that almost hides from my view the turbid, muddy waters of the creek in the gully, as it rolls furiously along. The thunder and thud of the batteries, the jarring and whirring of machinery, the bustle and stir of active and unceasing toil, reverberate with noisy clamour among the rocks, and proclaim that this stronghold of wild nature has been captured and occupied by man.

We four chums have not done well; indeed, we have done very badly. We have prospected our claim in all directions, but without success, and are now sinking a tunnel deep into the hill-side, in hopes of striking the reef that ought, we think, to run in a certain direction from where its upper levels are being successfully quarried in the prospectors' claim above us. We have stuck to the claim so far, urged by some fanciful belief not to give it up, and it bids fair to ruin us. Our funds are quite exhausted, and in another week we shall be compelled to give up the claim, to take work on wages here or at Grahamstown, and so raise means to get ourselves back to the Kaipara.

For the expenses have been great. What with buying provisions at frightful prices, buying implements and some bits of machinery, paying for the crushing of quartz that never yielded more than delusive traces of gold, and so on and so forth, our slender capital has melted away into nothingness. True, we have formed ourselves into a company, and have tried to sell some scrip. But the market is flooded with mining shares just now, and ours are not worth a bottle of whisky apiece. Moreover, "O'Gaygun's Claim" is fast becoming the laughing-stock of the field. There are no believers in it except ourselves. Every other claim that proved as valueless as ours has been long ago abandoned; only we stick to our tunnel, driving at it with frantic energy. And our life is harder here than in our shanty. We are ill-provided, and have all the wet and mud and mire of the rainy season now to help make things uncomfortable for us. Our food is coarse, and not too plentiful. Damper, tea, salt-pork, potatoes, and not always all of those. Is it any wonder we are despondent?

As I stand there that evening, cogitating over the gloomy outlook, two of the others come out of the tunnel bearing a sackful of stone between them. I see a new expression on their faces, and eagerly turn to them.

"Something fresh. Hush! Not a word. Come into the house, quick!"

So says Dandy Jack to me, hoarsely and hurriedly. Alas! poor man, he is hardly a dandy at present, and even his complacent calm seems to have forsaken him at last.

In the hut we anxiously crowd together, examining the specimens just brought out of the mine. There are lumps of grey and dirty-white quartz, flecked with little spots and speckles of metallic yellow. Is it gold? That is the question.

"Ah! it's just the same ould story!" growls O'Gaygun. "Mica or pyrites, that's about all we've the luck to find, bad cess to them! All's not gould that glitters, boys; an' there's precious little av the thrue stuff comin' our way."

"Shut up, you Irish croaker!" says Dandy Jack, without moving, as he lies on his face near the fire, intently examining a piece of quartz, licking it with his tongue, scratching it with his nails, and hefting it in his palms. "There's many a rough dirty stone that hides good gold within it. And," he adds, rising up, "we *have* got it this time. Boys! *we've struck the reef!*"

A few minutes later we were scouring down to the battery, bearing samples of the precious stone; and before the camp had gone to rest that night a hubbub and excitement had spread through it, for, it was the common topic of talk that rich stone had been discovered upon "O'Gaygun's Claim." Next day and next week we were besieged. Crowds wanted to see the claim, numbers wanted to buy shares in it, and would give hundreds and even thousands of pounds for them. We were elate, excited, conceited, madder than ever with our luck, that at last had come.

Well, eventually it proved that the find was but a "blind reef," a "pocket," a mere isolated dribble from the main continuous vein we had at first supposed we had struck. But it filled our pockets, giving us more wealth than we had ever before possessed. Had we been wiser we might have made more money by selling the claim directly after the find; but we held on too long. However, we made a very pretty little pile, not a fortune exactly, but the nucleus of one; and finally we sold the claim for a good round sum to a joint stock company, cleared out, and separated on the various ways we had chalked out for ourselves.

I find I can write no more, for many things are happening. O'Gaygun has set up as a stockbroker in Auckland, and will gamble away his share of our luck in gold-mine scrip. Dandy Jack has bought a large improved farm, and is collecting and importing a stud of brood mares. He is going to develop the equine resources of the colony. The Little'un has gone to Canterbury, intending to run sheep upon a large scale. And I am going to Australia and Fiji, perhaps home to England—who knows!

At Te Pahi amazing progress is taking place. A wharf is being constructed at the township, and a fine new steamer is being contracted for. Some new settlers have been tempted to come up into the district, and gangs of workmen are being hired from afar. A church has been subscribed for, and will soon be built. The Saint is erecting an hotel; and the Fiend is putting up a flour-mill. Old Colonial is going to get married, and a grand mansion, in the style of the Member's residence, is going up near the site of our shanty.

As I stand on the deck of the vessel that bears me away from New Zealand, I am filled with profound regrets at leaving the life I have grown to love so well. But it is not for long ; only for a season have I said farewell to the friends with whom I have toiled and struggled so long. I shall return some day, soon, to make my home in the beautiful land where the kauri grows. And the sun shines more brilliantly than ever upon the shores receding from my gaze, fit emblem of the prosperity of that glad new country, which we who love it like to call our " Brighter Britain."

APPENDIX.

SOME BOOKS ON NEW ZEALAND.

George F. Angas. "The New Zealanders." Folio. London. 1847.
A large collection of handsomely coloured plates.

"Rambles at the Antipodes." 8vo. London. 1859. Illustrated.
Contains a slight account of New Zealand, in addition to matter relating to Australia.

"The Australian Hand-book." (Gordon and Gotch.) London, Sydney, etc. 1881, and annually.
Extensive and varied information. Copious details of much value relating to New Zealand.

Lady M. A. Barker. "Station Life in New Zealand." London. 1871.
Description of home-life and experiences in Canterbury Province.

Alexander Bathgate. "Colonial Experiences." Glasgow. 1874.
Chiefly relates to Otago, and mining matters.

Alexander Bathgate. "Waitaruna; a Tale of New Zealand Life." London. 1881.

John Bathgate. (Judge.) "New Zealand; its Resources and Prospects." Edinburgh. 1880.
A useful summary of facts and figures.

C. D. Barraud. "New Zealand; Graphic and Descriptive." London. 1877. Illustrations by C. D. B. Letter-press by W. L. Travers. Folio.

An elaborately got up and beautiful album of New Zealand scenery. Coloured plates.

Beaven's "Narrative of a Voyage to New Zealand." London. 1842.

J. C. Bidwell. "Rambles in New Zealand." London. 1841.

One of the earliest recorded visits to the Lakes, the Hot-springs, and Tongariro.

S. C. Brees. "Pictorial Illustrations of New Zealand." London, 1846.

Walter Brodie. "Past and Present state of New Zealand." London. 1845.

W. Brown. "New Zealand and its Aborigines." London. 1845.

Brunner's "Journal of an Expedition into the Interior of the South Island." In the Geographical Society's "Proceedings." 1846.

B. received the Society's gold medal for this exploit.

"The Laws of England, compiled and translated into Maori." By desire of Governor Browne. Auckland. 1858.

Lord Brougham. "The New Zealanders." Published in Knight's Library of Entertaining Knowledge. London. 1830.

Edited by Lord B. Compiled from all the data available at that time. Contains the narrative of Rutherford, a sailor who lived among the Maoris. Has very quaint woodcuts.

James Busby. "Our Colonial Empire, and the Case of New Zealand." London. 1865.

The writer was British Resident for a short while before colonization in 1840. The book deals with governmental matters.

Rev. J. Berry. Narrative in "Constable's Miscellany." Vol. iv. London. 1820.

APPENDIX.

W. L. Buller, Sc.D. etc. "A History of the Birds of New Zealand." London. 1873. Quarto. Coloured plates.
The best and most complete work on New Zealand ornithology. Handsomely illustrating 145 species.

W. L. Buller, Sc.D. etc. An Essay on the "Ornithology of New Zealand." Published for the Commissioners of the New Zealand Exhibition. Dunedin. 1865.

Rev. Jas. Buller. "New Zealand, Past and Present." London. 1880.
A short historical sketch.

Chambers' "Emigrants' Manual." Edinburgh. 1849.
There have been more recent editions of this.

George T. Chapman. "Gazetteer of Auckland Province." Auckland. 1867.

G. T. Chapman. "The Traveller's Guide to New Zealand." Auckland. 1872.

G. T. Chapman. "The Circumnavigator. Cook Centenary." Auckland. 1870.
This volume is a creditable performance for the young publishing industries of the colony.

"A Chequered Career; or, Fifteen Years in Australia and New Zealand." London. 1881.
Amusing light reading.

The Church Missionary Society's Proceedings, Reports, and Publications. From 1814 and after. London.

"Captain Cook's Voyages."

A. Clayden. "The England of the Pacific." London. 1879.
Lectures, and letters furnished to the "Daily News." Illustrated.

An Old Colonist. "Colonial Experiences; or Incidents and Reminiscences of Thirty-four Years in New Zealand." London. 1877.
Some interesting details of early days in Wellington and Nelson.

APPENDIX.

J. C. Crawford. "Travels in New Zealand and Australia." London. 1880.
Of slight interest.

Major Richard A. Cruise. "Ten Months' Residence in New Zealand." London. 1823.
He commanded a detachment sent in charge of convicts to Tasmania, afterwards proceeding to New Zealand in the "Dromedary," which vessel had been despatched by the British Government to cut spars of kauri timber.

M. Crozet. "Nouveau Voyage à la Mer du Sud." Paris. 1805.
Contains an account of the massacre of Marion du Fresne and his people in 1772.

C. Darwin. "Voyage of a Naturalist." London. 1845.

E. Dieffenbach, M.D. "Travels in New Zealand." 2 vols. Illustrated. London. 1843.
This was considered the standard descriptive work until Dr. Hochstetter's book appeared and superseded it.

Sir Charles W. Dilke. "Greater Britain. A Record of Travel in English-speaking countries." London. 1868. 2 vols.
He visited New Zealand, among other places.

Dumont D'Urville. "Voyages dans l'Astrolabe." Paris. 1833.
Contains some excellent plates of New Zealand plants.

Augustus Earle. "Narrative of Nine Months' Residence in New Zealand" in 1827. London. 1832.
Readable. This author was inclined to be antagonistic to the early missionaries.

William Ellis. "Polynesian Researches." 5 vols. London. 1831.

Captain Fitzroy. "Voyages of the 'Adventure' and the 'Beagle.'" London. 1839.
Captain F. was subsequently Governor of New Zealand.

Sir William Fox. "The Six Colonies of New Zealand." London. 1851.
Sir William was at one time Premier of New Zealand and has recently received the honour of a baronetcy.

APPENDIX. 307

Sir William Fox. "The War in New Zealand." London. 1860 and 1866.

Captain F. Fuller. "Five Years' Residence in New Zealand." London. 1859.
The writer was a settler in Canterbury.

Sir George Grey. "Journal of Expedition overland from Auckland to Taranaki, in 1849." Auckland. 1851.

Sir G. Grey. "Ko Nga Moteatea, etc.—Poems and Chaunts of the Maori." Wellington. 1851.

Sir G. Grey. "Ko Nga Mahinga, etc.—Mythology and Traditions of the Maori." London. 1854.

Sir G. Grey. "Ko Nga Whakapehapeha, etc.—Proverbs and Sayings of the Maori." Capetown. 1857.

Sir G. Grey. "Maori Mementos." Auckland. 1855.

Sir G. Grey. "Polynesian Mythology, and Ancient Traditional History of the Maori Race." London. 1855.
Sir George is, perhaps, the best living master of the Maori tongue.

J. E. Gorst. "The Maori King." London. 1864.
The history of the Waikato War, admirably related.

John Gould. "Birds of Australia." 8 vols. Large folio. London. 1849–68.
The supplement to the eighth volume contains some of the New Zealand birds. They are accurately drawn and coloured, life-size. The same author's "Handbook of Birds of Australia" *contains scientific descriptions of some New Zealand species.*

Dr. J. Hann. "Meteorological Report, and Essay on the Climate of New Zealand." Colonial Meteorological Department. Wellington. 1874.

T. Heale. "New Zealand and the New Zealand Company." London. 1842.

Dr. J. Hector. "Reports." Geological Survey Department. Wellington. 1868, and since.

Dr. J. Hector, and E. von Martens. "Critical List of the Mollusca of New Zealand." Colonial Museum and Geological Survey Department. Wellington. 1873.

Dr. Ferdinand von Hochstetter. "New Zealand, its Physical Geography, Geology, and Natural History." Translated into English by E. Sauter. Stuttgart. 1867.
A valuable and standard work. Well illustrated in colours.

Sir Joseph D. Hooker. "The Botany of the Antarctic Voyage of H.M. Discovery Ships *Erebus* and *Terror*. Part II. Flora Novæ Zelandiæ." 2 vols. Quarto. London. 1853.
A splendidly illustrated work.

Sir J. D. Hooker. "Handbook of the New Zealand Flora." London. 1864.
The standard botanical work.

·W. Howitt. "The History of Discovery in Australia, Tasmania, and New Zealand." London. 1865. 2 vols.
The second volume contains some account of exploring expeditions in New Zealand.

Charles Hursthouse. "Account of the New Plymouth Settlement." London. 1849.

Charles Hursthouse. "New Zealand or Zealandia, the Britain of the South." London. 1857.
Copious information of a thoroughly reliable and practical sort. Racily written. The best book ever offered to possible emigrants.

F. W. Hutton. "The Tertiary Mollusca and Echinodermata of New Zealand." Colonial Museum and Geological Survey Department. Wellington. 1873.

F. W. Hutton. "Catalogue of the Echinodermata of New Zealand." With Diagnoses, etc. Colonial Museum and Geological Survey Department. Wellington. 1872.

F. W. Hutton and G. Hector. "The Fishes of New Zealand." Illustrated. Colonial Museum and Geological Survey Department. Wellington. 1872.
Good.

F. W. Hutton. "The Marine Mollusca of New Zealand." Colonial Museum and Geological Survey Department. Wellington. 1873.

"Land Mollusca of New Zealand." Collected from various authors. Colonial Museum and Geological Survey Department. Wellington. 1873.

J. Jameson. "New Zealand." London. 1842.

Lacy Kemp. "Pocket Vocabulary of Colloquial Maori and English." Auckland. 1848.

Alex. Kennedy. "New Zealand." London. 1874.
A capital history in brief.

Professor Lee (Cambridge). "Grammar of the Language of New Zealand," compiled from data furnished by Mr. Kendall, Hongi and Waikato. London. 1820.
Known as " Kendall's Grammar."

Judge Maning. "Old New Zealand; being Incidents of Native Customs and Character in the Old Times." By a Pakeha-Maori. London. 1863.
A stirring narrative of " the old days" of war and cannibalism.

Judge Maning. "Old New Zealand; together with a History of the War in the North against the Chief Heke, in 1845, as told by a Chief of the Ngapuhi." Edited by the Earl of Pembroke. London. 1876.
The addition is striking and characteristic.

A. Marjoribanks. "Travels in New Zealand." London. 1846.

Rev. Samuel Marsden. "Journal of Visits to New Zealand." London. 1822, etc.
Originally published in the C.M.S. "Proceedings." Mr. Marsden made five visits to New Zealand. He was the first to preach the gospel there.

Dr. S. M. D. Martin. "New Zealand, with Historical Remarks." London. 1845.

Rev. R. Maunsell. "Grammar of the New Zealand Language." Auckland. 1842. Revised edition, London. 1862.

APPENDIX.

Colonel Mundy. "Our Antipodes." 3 vols. London. 1852.
Vol. 3 contains an account of New Zealand.

D. L. Mundy. "The Southern Wonderland. Rotomahana, etc." A series of Photographic Views. Folio. London. 1875.
Very fine. There are other photographs published in London, besides those contained in this volume.

"The Natural Wonders of New Zealand." London. 1881.
A revised edition of Chapman's Guide. An historical and descriptive account of the Hot Lakes.

"The New Zealand Company's Reports." London. 1840–1858.
These are very copious.

John L. Nicholas. "Narrative of a Voyage to New Zealand." 2 vols. London. 1817.
An interesting account of the Rev. S. Marsden's first landing in New Zealand in 1814. The author went with the pioneer band of missionaries.

Commander R. A. Oliver. "Lithographic Drawings from Sketches in New Zealand." Folio. London. 1852.
Coloured pictures; fair, but not equal to Angas'.

"Outline of the Political and Physical Geography of Australia, Tasmania, and New Zealand." Collin's Series of School-books. London and Glasgow. 1876.

"Poenamo. Sketches of the early days of New Zealand." London. 1880.
Deals with Hauraki Gulf. Of very trifling interest.

J. S. Polack. "Travels in New Zealand." 2 vols. London. 1838.

J. S. Polack. "Manners and Customs of the New Zealanders." 2 vols. London. 1840. Illustrated.
Both Mr. Polack's books are very quaint and amusing.

G. S. Baden-Powell. "New Homes for the Old Country." London. 1872.
Mostly deals with Australian life, but also contains some New Zealand information.

APPENDIX.

W. T. Power. "Sketches of New Zealand." London. 1849.

Abbé Rochon. "Voyages aux Indes Orientales." Tom. iii. Paris. 1802.
Contains accounts of the voyages of the French explorers, De Bougainville, De Surville, Marion du Fresne, Crozet, and others.

Richard Rose. "The New Zealand Guide." London. 1879.
A little manual for intending emigrants. Gives some useful information.

"Robinson Crusoe," translated into Maori. Wellington. 1851.

E. Shortland. "The Southern Districts in New Zealand." London. 1851.

E. Shortland. "Traditions and Superstitions of the New Zealanders." London. 1854.

John Savage. "Some Account of New Zealand." London. 1807.
He visited the Bay of Islands, and brought home a Maori to England. Extremely interesting.

W. Swainson. "New Zealand and its Colonization." London. 1859.

W. Swainson. "New Zealand and the War." London. 1862.
Both books deal with details of law and government.

(S. W. Silver and Co.) "Handbook for Australia, New Zealand, and Fiji." London, etc. 1874.

Rev. Richard Taylor, F.G.S. "A Leaf from the Natural History of New Zealand." Auckland. 1848.

Rev. R. Taylor. "New Zealand and its Inhabitants." London. 1856.

Rev. R. Taylor. "The Past and Present of New Zealand." London. 1868.

Rev. R. Taylor. "Te Ika a Maui." London. 1870.
This is the best of Mr. Taylor's books, containing a very exhaustive and

studious account of old Maori manners and customs. All his books are good; but missionary class prejudice is occasionally somewhat strong in the others.

Rev. R. Taylor. "Maori-English Dictionary." Auckland. 1870.

Charles Terry. "New Zealand, its Advantages and Prospects." London. 1842.
Refers to Auckland.

Arthur S. Thomson, M.D. "The Story of New Zealand, Past and Present, Savage and Civilized." 2 vols. London. 1859. Illustrated.
A good and valuable work. A standard authority on the history of the wars between the first settlers and the Maoris. Appended is a Catalogue of New Zealand bibliography down to 1859, fairly full and accurate.

Mrs. C. Thomson. "Twelve Years in Canterbury, New Zealand; from a Lady's Journal." London. 1867.
Small details of home life and personal matters.

Anthony Trollope. "New Zealand." London. 1874.
The result of a rapid tour through the Colony.

Miss Tucker. "The Southern Cross and the Southern Crown, or the Early History of the Gospel in New Zealand." London. 1855.
A big title, but a little book.

Sir Julius Vogel. "Great Britain and her Colonies." London. 1865.

Sir Julius Vogel. "New Zealand and the South Sea Islands, and their Relation to the Empire." London. 1878.
Deals with the author's great scheme of federation and colonization, enunciated by him when Premier of New Zealand.

Sir Julius Vogel. "The Official Handbook of New Zealand." Papers by various hands, collected and edited by Sir Julius Vogel. With illustrations and maps. London. 1875.
The best and latest compilation of the kind.

APPENDIX. 313

Sir Julius Vogel. "Land and Farming in New Zealand." Information respecting the mode of acquiring land; with particulars as to farming, wages, prices, etc. Also the Land Acts of 1877, and maps.
> *Contains very good maps. This, together with the Handbook, are published at the New Zealand Government offices in London, and are designed to furnish every information to all classes of inquirers.*

E. Jerningham Wakefield. "Adventures in New Zealand." 2 vols. London. 1845.
> *Interesting. Together with it was published a volume of sketches and views.*

E. Jerningham Wakefield. "Handbook of New Zealand." London. 1848.

The Wellington Chamber of Commerce. "Annual Reports." Wellington. 1864, etc.

The Wesleyan Missionary "Reports." London. 1820, and since. Also, from the same date, various publications of the Society for Promoting Christian Knowledge; of the Aborigines' Protection Society; of the London Missionary Society; and, the "Missionary Register."

Whateley's "Easy Letters on Money Matters," translated into Maori. Wellington. 1851.

Rev. John Williams. "A Narrative of Missionary Enterprises." London. 1838.

Rev. W. Williams (Bishop of Waiapu). "A Dictionary and Grammar of the New Zealand Language." Auckland. 1844.
> *Later and improved editions have been published in London, in 1852 and 1871.*

Ven. W. L. Williams. "First Lessons in Maori." London. 1872.

N.B. I cannot claim that the above list is a complete one. It is not. It merely contains the books I have been able to come across. Dr. Thomson compiled a careful list of all publications relating to New Zealand down to the year 1859. Such a task would be very much more arduous now, and the result would not repay the trouble bestowed on it. There have been, both before and since 1859, shoals of pamphlets bearing on matters connected with the colony. Since that year, too, the periodical literature of Great Britain, Australia, the United States, and other countries, has contained countless articles on New Zealand subjects. Finally, "Brighter Britain" has now a literature of its own. Its press and its publishers are busy. Yet, I think, that in the foregoing catalogue will be found all, or nearly all, the substantial volumes immediately relating to New Zealand that the general reader, or particular inquirer, need care to become acquainted with.

APPENDIX.

THE NEW ZEALAND PRESS.

Name of Town.	Population according to Census and estimates 1879-80.		Title of Newspaper or Journal.	Issue.	County in which the Town is situated.	Former Province.
	Population of Town.	Population of Town and District.				
Auckland	13,758	31,401	The Southern Cross	Daily	Eden	Auckland
			The New Zealand Herald	,,		
			The Evening Star	,,		
			The Weekly News	Weekly		
			The Weekly Herald	,,		
			The Saturday Night	,,		
			The Presbyterian Church News	Monthly		
			The Church Gazette	,,		
			The New Zealand Almanac	Annually		
Coromandel	2,053	—	The Coromandel Mail	Tri-weekly	Coromandel	Auckland
			The Coromandel News	,,		
Grahamstown, *with Shortland*	5,424	10,423	The Thames Advertiser	Daily	Thames	Auckland
			The Thames Evening Star	,,		
			The Thames Exchange	Weekly		
			Enoch	,,		
Gisborne	1,204	—	The Poverty Bay Standard	Bi-weekly	Cook	Auckland
			The Poverty Bay Herald	Daily		
Kororareka *(Russell)*	329	—	The Northern Luminary	Weekly	Bay of Islands	Auckland

APPENDIX.

Name of Town.	Population of Town.	Population of Town and District.	Title of Newspaper or Journal.	Issue.	County in which the Town is situated.	Former Province.
Whangarei	1,288	2,906	The Whangarei Comet and Northern Advocate	Weekly	Whangarei	Auckland
Hamilton	1,243	—	The Waikato Times	Tri-weekly	Waikato	Auckland
Ngaruawahia (*Newcastle*)	277	—	The Waikato News	,,	Waipa	Auckland
Tauranga	793	2,770	The Bay of Plenty Times	Weekly	Tauranga	Auckland
New Plymouth	2,678	—	The Taranaki Herald	Bi-weekly	Taranaki	Taranaki
			The Taranaki News	Weekly		
			The Evening Budget	Daily		
Wairoa (*Clyde*)	120	—	The Wairoa Free Press	Weekly	Wairoa	Hawke's Bay
Napier	6,550	—	The Hawke's Bay Herald	Daily	Hawke's Bay	Hawke's Bay
			The Hawke's Bay Telegraph	,,		
			The Hawke's Bay Times	Bi-weekly		
			The Hawke's Bay Weekly Courier	Weekly		
			The Hawke's Bay Weekly Telegraph	,,		
			The Hawke's Bay Weekly Mercury	Daily		
			The Hawke's Bay Evening Star	Weekly		
			Te Wananga (*Maori*)			
WELLINGTON	18,953	21,005	The New Zealand Times	Daily	Hutt	Wellington
			The Wellington Independent	,,		
			The Wellington Tribune	,,		

APPENDIX. 317

		The New Zealand Mail	Weekly	Wellington
		The New Zealander	,,	Wellington
		The Illustrated New Zealand News	Fortnightly	Wellington
		Te Waka Maori (*Maori*)	Monthly	Wellington
		The New Zealand Magazine	,,	Wellington
		The New Zealand Bradshaw	,,	Wellington
		The Church Chronicle	,,	Wellington
		The New Zealand Quarterly Review	Quarterly	Wellington
Greytown	1,400	The Wairarapa Standard	Bi-weekly	Wairarapa West
Carterton	446	The Wairarapa Guardian	,,	Wairarapa West
Masterton	1,673	The Wairarapa Daily	Daily	Wairarapa West
Palmerston (*North*)	880	The Manawatu Times	Weekly	Manawatu
Foxton	563	The Manawatu Herald	,,	Manawatu
Wanganui	4,163	The Wanganui Chronicle	Daily	Wanganui
	7,744	The Wanganui Evening Herald	,,	
		The Weekly Chronicle	Weekly	
		The Weekly Herald	,,	
Carlyle	405	The Patea Mail	,,	Patea
Hawera	500	The Hawera and Normanby Star	,,	Patea
Marton	850	The Rangitikei Advocate	,,	Rangitikei
Nelson	6,804	The Nelson Times	Daily	Waimea
	8,810	The Nelson Evening Mail	,,	
		The Nelson Colonist	Tri-weekly	
Westport	1,166	The Buller News	Daily	Buller
	1,800			

APPENDIX.

Westport	...	—	The Westport Evening Star ...	Daily	Buller... ...	Nelson
			The Westport Times ...	,,		
Charleston	...	185	The Charleston Herald ...	Bi-weekly	Buller... ...	Nelson
			The Charleston News ...	Weekly		
Reefton	...	1,031	The Inangahua Courier ...	Daily	Inangahua ...	Nelson
			The Inangahua Herald ...	Tri-weekly		
			The Inangahua Times ...	,,		
Lyell	...	250	The Lyell Argus	Bi-weekly	Buller... ...	Nelson
Blenheim	...	1,701	The Marlborough Express ...	Daily	Marlborough...	Marlborough
			The Marlborough Times ...	,,		
			The Weekly Express ...	Weekly		
			The Weekly Times ...	,,		
Kaikoura	...	200	The Kaikoura Herald	,,	Kaikoura ...	Marlborough
Picton...	...	703	The Marlborough Press ...	,,	Sounds ...	Marlborough
Hokitika	...	3,203	The West Coast Times ...	Daily	Westland ...	Westland
			The Evening Star	,,		
			The Westland Register ...	Weekly		
			The Leader ...	,,		
Greymouth	...	2,921	The Grey River Argus ...	Daily	Grey	Westland
			The Greymouth Star	,,		

APPENDIX. 319

Ross ...	1,068	—	The Ross Guardian ...	Tri-weekly	Westland
Lyttelton ...	3,653	—	The Lyttelton Times ...	Daily	Selwyn ...	Canterbury
			The Lyttelton Evening Star ...	"	
			The Lyttelton Globe ...	Weekly	
			The Canterbury Times ...	"	
			The Canterbury Illustrated Press ...	"	
Christchurch ...	15,156	32,031	The Canterbury Press ...	Daily	Selwyn ...	Canterbury
			The Evening Globe	"	
			The Weekly Press ...	Weekly	
			The New Zealand Sun ...	"	
			The Illustrated News	"	
			The New Zealand Presbyterian ...	Monthly	
			The New Zealand Church News	"	
			Te Mokomaka (*Maori*) ...	"	
			The New Zealand Wesleyan ...	"	
			The Licensed Victuallers' Gazette ...	"	
Kaiapoi ...	1,083	6,284	The North Canterbury News ...	Daily	Ashley ...	Canterbury
Rangiora ...	—	2,888	The North Canterbury News	"	Ashley ...	Canterbury
Akaroa ...	642	2,232	The Akaroa Mail	Weekly	Akaroa ...	Canterbury
Ashburton ...	1,200	—	The Ashburton Mail ...	Daily	Ashburton ...	Canterbury
			The Evening Herald	"	
			The Ashburton Guardian ...	Weekly	
Te Muka ...	200	—	Te Muka Herald	"	Geraldine ...	Canterbury
Timaru ...	3,791	—	The Timaru Herald ...	Daily	Geraldine ...	Canterbury
			The South Canterbury Times ...	"	
			The Evening Telegraph ...	"	
			The Geraldine Chronicle	Weekly	

Name of Town.	Population according to Census and estimates 1879-80.		Title of Newspaper or Journal.	Issue.	County in which the Town is situated.	Former Province.
	Population of Town.	Population of Town and District.				
Waiemate ...	—	4,269	The Waiemate Times The Waietangi Tribune	Bi-weekly ,,	Waiemate	Canterbury
Dunedin ...	23,959	34,674	The Otago Times The Otago Morning Herald The Otago Guardian The Otago Evening Tribune The Otago Evening Star The Otago Witness The Otago Southern Mercury The Christian Record The Otago Penny Post The Age The New Zealand Tablet (R.C.) The Saturday Advertiser The New Zealand News The Illustrated New Zealand Herald The New Zealand Temperance Herald The New Zealand Churchman The New Zealand Presbyterian	Daily ,, ,, ,, ,, Weekly ,, ,, ,, ,, ,, ,, ,, Monthly ,, ,,	Taieri	Otago

APPENDIX.

Lawrence	...	855	5,400	The Weekly Times The Weekly News	Weekly "
				The Tuapeka Times	Bi-weekly	Tuapeka ...	Otago
Tapanui	...	335	—	The Tapanui Courier	Weekly	Tuapeka ...	Otago
Tokomairiro (*Milton*)	...	1,161	—	The Bruce Herald The Bruce Standard ...	Bi-weekly "	Bruce	Otago
Naseby	...	546	—	The Mount Ida Chronicle	Weekly	Maniatoto ...	Otago
Balclutha	...	900	—	The Clutha Mail	"	Clutha ...	Otago
Oamaru	...	5,098	—	The North Otago Times ... The Oamaru Evening Mail The North Otago Weekly Times The Oamaru Weekly Mail	Daily " Weekly "	Waitaki ...	Otago
Palmerston	...	825	—	The Shag Valley Herald ... The Waikouaiti Times	" "	Waikouaiti ...	Otago
Arrowtown	...	363	—	The Arrow Observer	"	Lake	Otago
Queenstown	...	574	2,266	The Wakatipu Mail ...	"	Lake	Otago
Riverton	...	867	4,194	The Western Star	"	Wallace ...	Otago

I must apologize for any omissions or inaccuracies that may be found to appear in the above list. The materials were not collected without considerable trouble, and every care has been taken to ensure fulness. The figures are derived from returns published according to the census and estimates of 1879 and 1880. Their incompleteness was unavoidable.

VOL. II.   43

POPULATION OF NEW ZEALAND.

European. In 1844 the total European population was 13,128
,, 1851 ,, ,, ,, 26,707
,, 1856 ,, ,, ,, 45,540
,, 1861 ,, ,, ,, 99,021
,, 1866 ,, ,, ,, 204,114
,, 1871 ,, ,, ,, 256,393
,, 1874 ,, ,, ,, 299,684
,, 1879-80 ,, ,, ,, 463,729

Maori. In 1820 the total Maori population was 100,000 (supposed).
,, 1874 ,, ,, ,, 46,016
,, 1879-80 ,, ,, ,, 42,819

The present total population of all New Zealand, both of Europeans and Maoris, may be set down at 506,548.

POLITICAL DIVISIONS.

In 1876, the old provincial divisions, with all their cumbrous local governments and legislative machinery, were finally abolished. Politically speaking, therefore, the provinces of Auckland, Taranaki, Hawke's Bay, Wellington, Nelson, Marlborough, Canterbury, Otago, and Westland no longer exist. The names are still retained to some extent in general use, but they will probably pass away as the new arrangement takes deeper hold. The colony is now divided into sixty-three counties, which are here enumerated, together with the three principal cities, towns, villages, or settlements comprised within each. The arrangement is from North to South.

County.	Towns or Settlements.
Mongonui ...	Mongonui, Whangaroa, Ahipara.
Hokianga ...	Hokianga, Whangape, Kaikohe.
Bay of Islands	Kororareka, Kawakawa, Waimate.
Whangarei ...	Whangarei, Mangapai, Waipu.
Hobson ...	Tokatoka, Aratapu, Pahi.
Rodney ...	Mangawai, Omaha, Mahurangi.
Waitemata ...	Helensville, Whangaparoa, Riverhead.

APPENDIX.

County.	Towns or Settlements.
Eden	AUCKLAND, Onehunga, Otahuhu.
Manukau	Waiuku, Papakura, Pukekohe.
Coromandel	Port Fitzroy, Kapanga, Tokatea.
Thames	Grahamstown, Tairua, Ohinemuri.
Waikato	Mercer, Hamilton, Cambridge.
Waipa	Ngaruawahia, Te Awamutu, Alexandra.
Raglan	Raglan, Port Waikato.
Piako	Piako.
Tauranga	Tauranga, Maketu, Ohinemutu.
Kawhia	Kawhia, Aotea, Kuiti.
West Taupo	Orakau, Tokano.
East Taupo	Tapuaeharuru, Cox's.
Whakatane	Opotiki, Whakatane, Matata.
Cook	Gisborne, Ormond, Uawa.
Wairoa	Mahia, Clyde, Mohaka.
Hawke's Bay	NAPIER, Hastings, Havelock.
Wanganui	Wanganui, Makirikiri, Kai Iwi.
Taranaki	NEW PLYMOUTH, Oakura, Raleigh.
Patea	Carlyle, Hawera, Normanby.
Rangitikei	Bulls, Marton, Turakina.
Manawatu	Foxton, Palmerston, Fielding.
Waipawa	Waipawa, Waipukerau, Wallingford.
Wairarapa East	Akiteo, Mataikuna, Whareama.
Wairarapa West	Featherston, Greytown, Masterton.
Hutt	WELLINGTON, Hutt, Karori.
Collingwood	Collingwood, Clifton, Takaka.
Waimea	NELSON, Wakefield, Foxhill.
Sounds	Picton, Gore, Bulwer.
Marlborough	BLENHEIM, Renwick, Tuamarina.
Inangahua	Reefton, Howard, Hampden.
Buller	Westport, Charleston, Lyell.
Grey	Greymouth, Cobden, Ahaura.
Amuri	Waiau, Hanmer Bridge, Tarndale.
Kaikoura	Kaikoura, Hapuka, Clarence.
Cheviot	Cheviot, Hawkswood.
Ashley	Kaiapoi, Rangiora, West Oxford.
Akaroa	Wairewa, Akaroa.
Selwyn	CHRISTCHURCH, Lyttelton, Selwyn.
Westland	HOKITIKA, Ross, Kumara.
Ashburton	Ashburton, Rangitata, Rakaia.
Geraldine	Timaru, Geraldine, Te Muka.
Waiemate	Waiemate, Makikihi, Waihoa.
Waitaki	Oamaru, Herbert, Moeraki.

County.	Towns or Settlements.
Waikouaiti ...	... Palmerston, Waikouaiti, Port Chalmers.
Peninsula ...	Calversham, Tairoa.
Taieri ...	... DUNEDIN, Outram, Berwick.
Maniatoto ...	Naseby, St. Bathans, Hamilton.
Vincent ...	... Clyde, Cromwell, Gladstone.
Lake ...	... Queenstown, Arrowtown, Cardrona.
Fiord ...	... (No settlement).
Wallace ...	Riverton, Wallace, Howells.
Southland ...	... Invercargill, Dacre, Athol.
Tuapeka ...	Lawrence, Tapanui, Roxburgh.
Bruce ...	... Milton, Kaitangata, Waihora.
Clutha ...	Balclutha, Clinton, Waipaheu.
Stewart Island	... Paterson.

PRONUNCIATION OF MAORI NAMES.

THE letters of the Maori Alphabet are only fourteen in number. They are—a, e, h, i, k, m, n, ng, o, p, r, t, u, w. The vowels have an Italian sound.

The Maori a is pronounced like aw and ah.
,, e ,, ,, a and eh.
,, i ,, ,, ee.
,, o ,, ,, o and oo (short).
,, u ,, ,, oo (long).

When two vowels come together in a syllable, both are pronounced in a single breath. Thus :—

The Maori au becomes ow, as in *cow*.
,, ao the same.
,, ae becomes i, as in *sigh*.
,, ai the same.
,, ei becomes ee, as in *keep*.

Ng always has a nasal sound, as in *ringing*. G is never hard.

In common use among colonists, many names are becoming corrupted, principally by the shortening of vowel sounds. Thus,

APPENDIX.

Wakatipu, the proper pronunciation of which should be Waw-kahtee'-poo, has become Wacky-tip. The elision of a final vowel in certain instances, is common among the Maori themselves. The following examples, selected from names occurring in this book, may be of use. Chief stress is to be laid upon the syllable indicated by an accent mark.

Arapaoa	Ah-rah-pow'-ah	Kumera	Koo'-meh-rah
Ararimu	Ah-rah-ree'-moo	Mahurangi	Mow'-ă-rang'-ee
Aratapu	Ah-rah-tah'-poo	Maire	Mi'-ray
Ariki	Ah-ree'-kee	Manukau	Man'-oo-kow
Atua	Ah'-too-ah	Mangapai	Mong'-ah-pi
Hauraki	How'-rah-kee	Mangawai	Mong-ah-wi'
Hinau	Hee'-now	Mangiao	Mong-ee-ow'
Hokianga	Ho-kee-ang'-ah	Maori	Mow'-ree
Hone Heke	Ho'-nay Hek'-ky	Matakohe	Mah-tah-ko'-eh
Hongi Hika	Hong'-ee Hee'-kah	Marahemo	Mah-rah-hay'-mo
Hoteo	Ho-tay'-o	Maungakahia	Mong-ah-ki'-ah
Hue	Hoo'-eh	Mihake	Mee'-hak-ă
Kahikatea	Ki-kah-tay'-ah	Mongonui	Mong-o-noo'-ee
Kai	Ki	Ngapuhi	Ng-ah'-poo-ee
Kainga	Ki'-ng-ah	Ngatewhatua	Ng-ah'-tay-whot'-oo-ah
Kaipara	Ki'-pah-rah		
Kamahi	Kah-mi'	Ohaeawae	O-hi'-ah-wi
Kapai	Kah'-pi	Okaehau	O-ki'-how
Kapuka	Kah'-poo-kah	Onehunga	O-nay-hung'-ah
Kararehe	Kah-rah'-ray	Otamatea	O-tah-mah-tay'-ah
Kareao	Kah-ray-ow'	Oruawharo	Or-oo-ah-whah'-ro
Kauri	Kow'-ree	Pahi	Pah'-hee
Kawa	Kaw'-ah	Paparoa	Pah-pah-ro'-ah
Kawau	Kah-wow'	Pakeha	Pah'-kay-hah
Kawiti	Kaw'-ee-tee	Pohutukawa	Paw'-tah-kow-ah
Keri-keri	Kirry-kirry	Ponamu	Po-nam'-oo
Kiwi	Kee'-wee	Puna	Poo'-nah
Kihi-kihi	Kēē-kēē	Puriri	Poo-ry'-ry
Kiore	Kee-or'-eh	Rakope	Raw'-kop-ă
Kopura	Ko'-poo-rah	Rangatira	Rang-ah-tee'-rah
Koraka	Ko-rah'-kah	Rangitopuni	Rang-ee-to-poo'-nee
Korero	Kor'-ră-ro	Raupo	Row'-poo
Kororareka	Kor-or-ar'-ek-ah	Reinga	Ray-eeng'-ah
Kotuku	Ko-too'-koo	Rimu	Ree'-moo
Kowhai	Ko'-i	Taheke	Tah'-hak-ky

APPENDIX.

Tamatewhiti	Tom'-ah-tay-whee'-tee	Waimate	Wi'-matty
Taupo	Tow'-poo	Waitangi	Wi'-tang-ee
Tawhera	Taff'-rah	Waitemata	Wi'-tay-mah'-tah
Taua	Tow'-ah	Whangarei	Whong-ah-ree'
Tapu	Tah'-poo	Whare	Whah'-ray
Te	Tay	Whau	Whow
Ti	Tee	Wairoa	Wi'-raw
Wahine	Wah-hee'-nay	Wairau	Wi'-row

THE END.

www.ingramcontent.com/pod-product-compliance
Lightning Source LLC
Chambersburg PA
CBHW021205230426
43667CB00006B/565